Introducing European Tapestries

Rebecca Quinton

First published in 2022 by Glasgow Museums Publishing.
Text © Culture and Sport Glasgow (Museums) 2022.
Images © CSG CIC Glasgow Museums Collection, unless otherwise acknowledged.

ISBN 978-1-908638-33-5

Written by Rebecca Quinton
Edited by Fiona MacLeod
Designed by Jacqui Duffus
Photography by Enzo di Cosmo and Ellen Howden
Images supplied by Glasgow Museums Photo Library
www.csgimages.org.uk
www.glasgowmuseums.com

Front cover image: detail from *Birds and Beasts in a Landscape with a Mille-Fleurs Ground: Wyvern and Griffin*, about 1525, 46.105
Back cover image: detail from *Fight Between a Falcon and a Heron*, about 1525, 46.60

Acknowledgements

All efforts have been made to trace copyright holders, but if any omissions have been made inadvertently, please contact the publishers.
Thanks to Dr Elizabeth Cleland, Dr Lorraine Karafel and Elizabeth Hancock.

Printed in Scotland by J Thomson Colour Printers, Glasgow
Cover printed on 350gsm Galerie Satin; text printed on 150gsm Galerie Satin

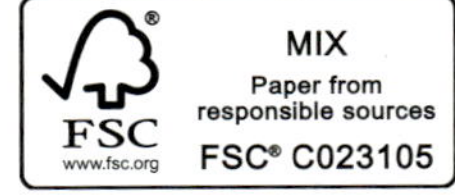

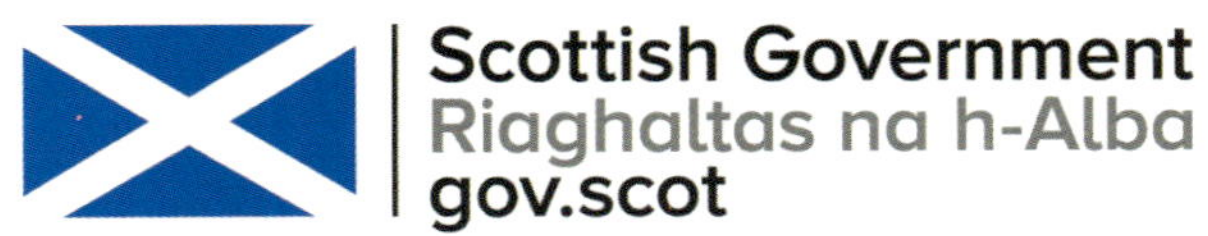

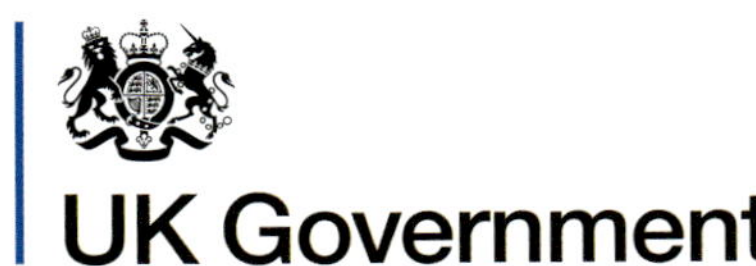

Contents

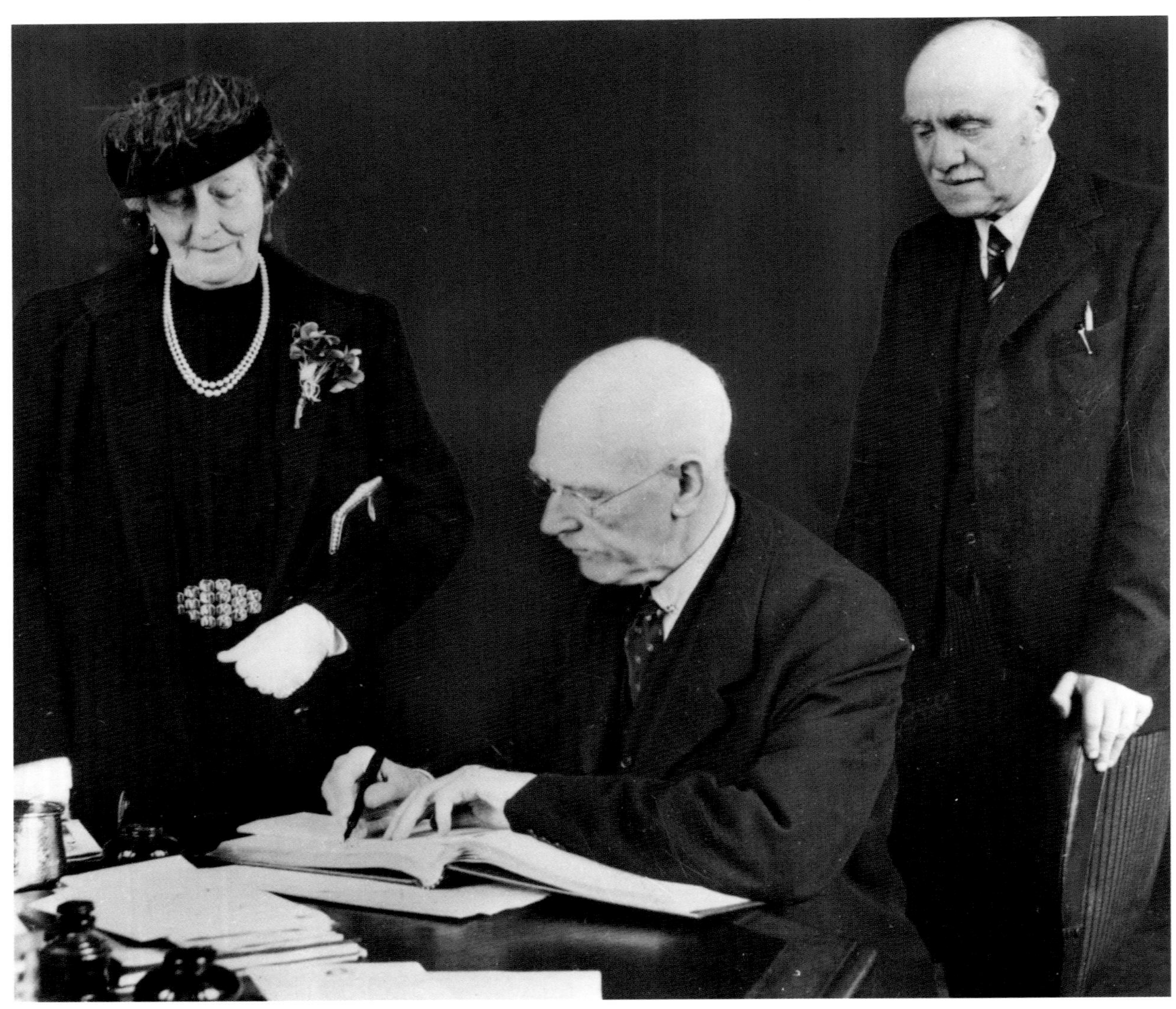

Sir William Burrell (seated), Constance, Lady Burrell and
Lord Provost James Welsh at the City Chambers, Glasgow,
1944, on the occasion of Sir William receiving the Freedom
of the City of Glasgow. Glasgow Museums Archive,
GMA.2013.1.1.470.

The Burrell Collection: The Gift of Sir William and Constance, Lady Burrell

The Burrell Collection comprises over 9,000 objects gifted to the city of Glasgow by Sir William Burrell (1861–1958) and his wife Constance, Lady Burrell (1875–1961). The main gift, of around 6,000 objects, was in 1944, but Burrell continued to add to it until his death, and the Collection has been further augmented with funds gifted by Burrell and administered by the Burrell Trustees.

Sir William made his fortune in shipping at a time when Glasgow was second city of the Empire. Collecting was a lifelong passion, and his treasures adorned his various homes: archive photographs show tapestries, sculpture, paintings and furniture in his house in Great Western Terrace, Glasgow. These, and also ceramics, stained glass, arms and armour and textiles, were displayed at Hutton Castle, his home in the Scottish Borders.

A sophisticated collector with a discerning eye, Burrell appreciated fine craftsmanship and meticulous attention to detail. From tapestries to sculpture, nineteenth-century French art to Chinese bronzes, medieval stained glass to Islamic carpets, the breadth and quality of his collection demonstrate his wide-ranging embrace of different cultures and art forms. Sir William also gave money for a new building to house his collection, and it is now displayed in a purpose-built museum in the centre of Pollok Country Park, on the south side of Glasgow. The park was gifted to the city in 1967 by Mrs Anne Maxwell Macdonald (1906–2011), and a competition, sponsored by the Royal Institute of British Architects, was held to design a suitable building within it to house the Collection. The winners of the competition, architects Barry Gasson, John Meunier and Brit Andresen, came up with a building which not only displays the Collection to advantage, but is also in harmony with the surrounding parkland. The building opened in 1983, but through the decades the Scottish weather took its toll and in 2016 the Category-A listed building closed for an ambitious programme of refurbishment, redisplay and reinterpretation.

This series is designed to introduce different parts of the Collection. Written by subject specialists, each book gives an insight into the Burrell's treasures. We, the Trustees of The Burrell Collection, are delighted to see the amount of new research that has been carried out on the objects in the collection, and hope that visitors will continue to enjoy Sir William and Constance, Lady Burrell's gift for many generations to come.

Professor Frances Fowle
Senior Trustee, Sir William Burrell's Trust

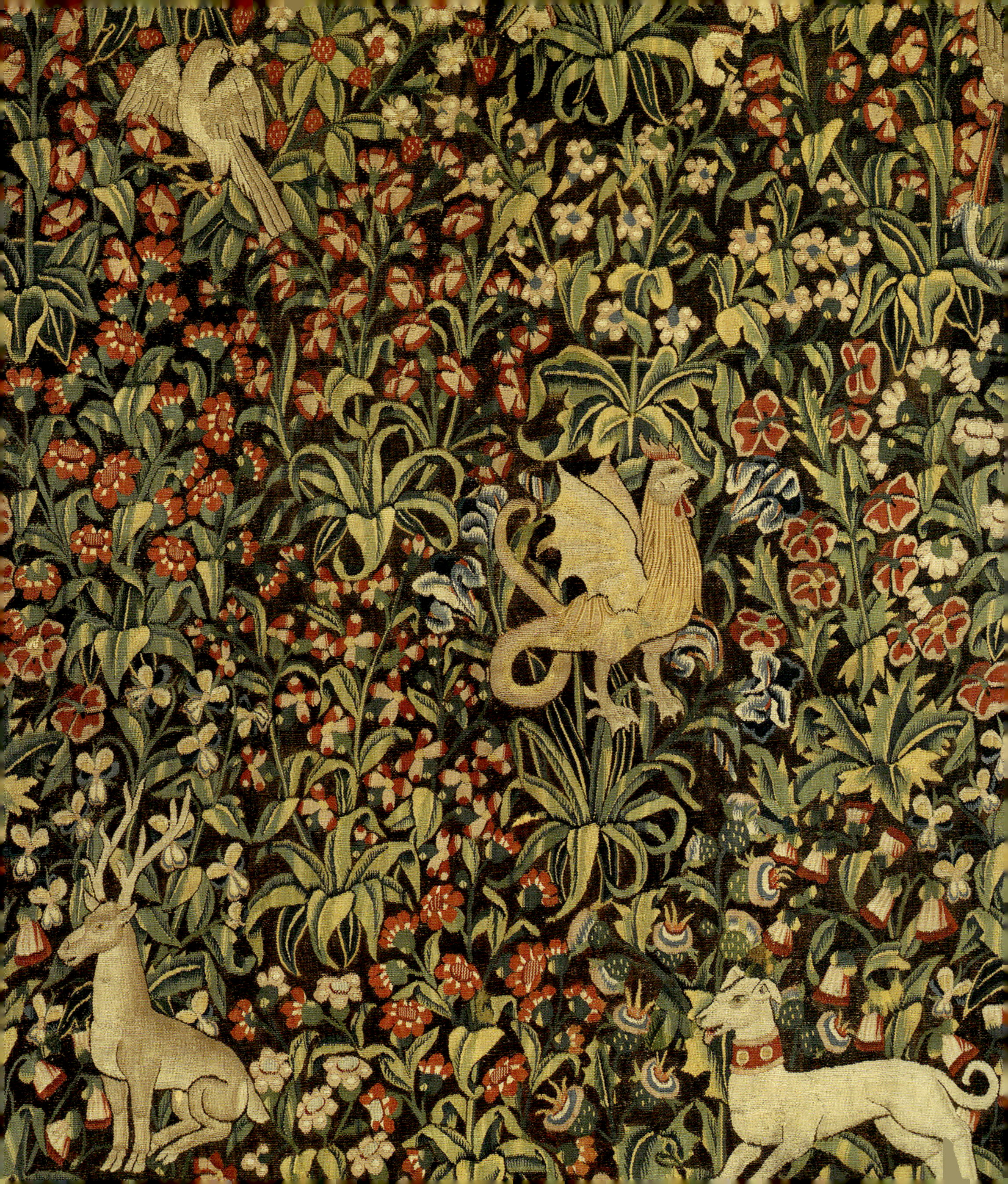

Introduction

Tapestries were one of the major interests of Sir William Burrell. Over a period of more than 60 years he bought over 200 tapestries made in medieval and Renaissance Europe. This not only included majestic French and South Netherlandish tapestries commissioned by kings, princes and bishops, but also smaller domestic tapestries woven in Alsace, Germany and England for the emerging wealthy merchant classes.

Burrell and his wife, Constance *née* Mitchell, decorated their homes extensively with tapestries. Photographs of 8 Great Western Terrace, Glasgow, taken in 1902, show several of their early purchases hung or mounted on the walls. In 1916 Burrell bought Hutton Castle, near Berwick-upon-Tweed, in the Scottish Borders. As well as showcasing tapestries in the principal reception rooms, such as the hall and drawing room, they also decorated the walls of the private family rooms with them.

Sir William Burrell was a generous lender. Both he and his mother lent tapestries to the Glasgow International Exhibition in 1901. Other early loans were to exhibitions in Glasgow and Edinburgh, but later Burrell lent to major museums, colleges and cathedrals in England, culminating in the decision to gift the entire collection to the city of Glasgow in 1944.

The word 'tapestry' derives from the Latin term *tapis*, meaning 'heavy fabric'. Today the terms 'tapestry' and 'embroidery' are often used interchangeably. *The Bayeux Tapestry*, made to celebrate the Norman Conquest of England in 1066, is embroidered with stitches applied to a pre-woven cloth. However, the term 'tapestry' is also used more specifically to describe hangings and panels where the design is woven into the fabric as it is made on the loom.

Tapestries are traditionally hand-woven back-to-front on looms. To begin, long warp threads are fixed and tensioned on opposite ends of the loom, normally vertically. Behind the loom is placed a full-scale drawing of the design, known as a cartoon. The key lines of the design may be traced onto the warp threads to guide the weaver, but the details are copied from sight or memory. Weavers use multiple weft threads in a variety of colours, each shade woven individually, to reproduce the design. The majority of medieval and Renaissance tapestries were woven on their side. This meant that the maximum height of the final tapestry was set by the width of the loom. However, if the warp threads were fixed on rotating poles at each end, the tapestry could be made wider by turning them regularly as it was woven.

Opposite: This tapestry is one of six tapestries purchased by Sir William Burrell that were owned previously by American businessman and newspaper owner, William Randolph Hearst (1863–1951). *Birds and Beasts in a Landscape with a Mille-Fleurs Ground: Wyvern and Griffin* (detail; see also p. 55).

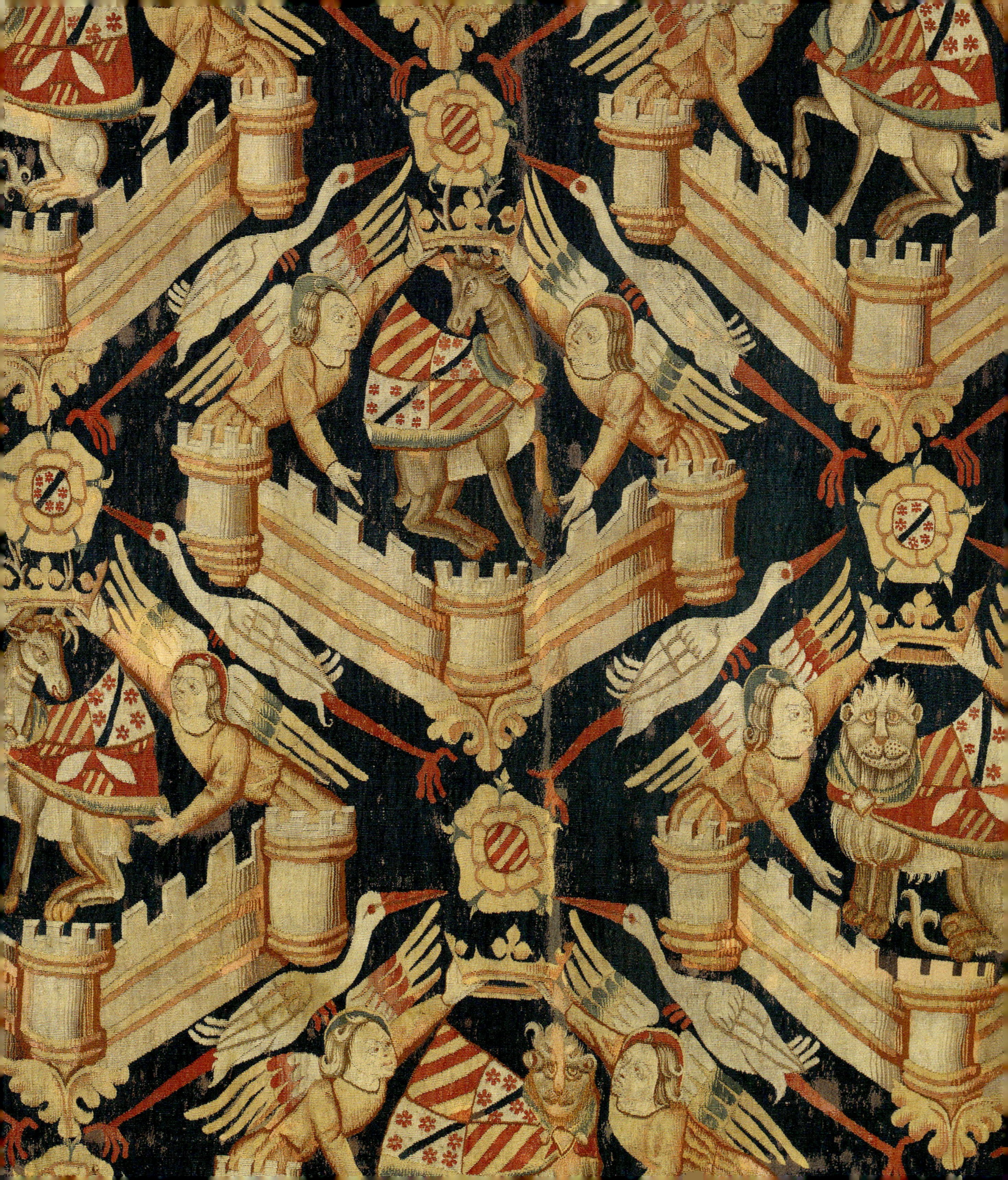

Fourteenth-century Tapestries

Only the very wealthiest people could afford to buy tapestries. During the Middle Ages the most expensive items made were gold and silver plate, followed by textiles, especially tapestries. Weaving a complex and detailed design is time-consuming, with the largest tapestries taking a number of highly skilled weavers a few years to complete. Once the cost of the raw materials was added in, particularly if the tapestry had a high silk content or metal threads, only the very wealthiest people could afford to buy them. As a result early medieval tapestries were made exclusively for well-funded religious institutions, aristocrats and rulers.

At this date tapestries had active lives. Often they were displayed for specific court or religious occasions, then taken down, rolled up and put away until the next time they were needed. As precious possessions they were moved with their owners between palaces, castles and hunting lodges, and with them went dedicated servants to care for them, carefully mending them as and when required. These people played their part towards ensuring that many tapestries would survive the following centuries.

The nineteenth century saw a revival of interest in medieval art and architecture. New buildings and tapestries were made in the Gothic Revival style, while surviving historical tapestries were bought and displayed by leading museums, including the South Kensington Museum, now the Victoria and Albert Museum, London, which William Burrell visited regularly. It is not known what initially sparked Burrell's interest, but from the correspondence of his friend Robert Lorimer (1864–1929) it is clear that he was buying tapestries from the 1890s onwards. One of Lorimer's letters, dated 12 February 1898, states that Burrell 'travels pretty well all over Europe 2 or 3 times a year visiting agents'. Over the following 60 years Burrell developed his knowledge, buying a number of leading reference books and visiting museums as well as dealers in Britain and Europe.

Opposite: Guillaume III Rogier de Beaufort commissioned a number of tapestries that may have been used to create a 'chambre' with matching wall hangings, bed hangings and bench covers. *Armorial Tapestry of Beaufort, Turenne and Comminges* (detail; see also p. 12–13).

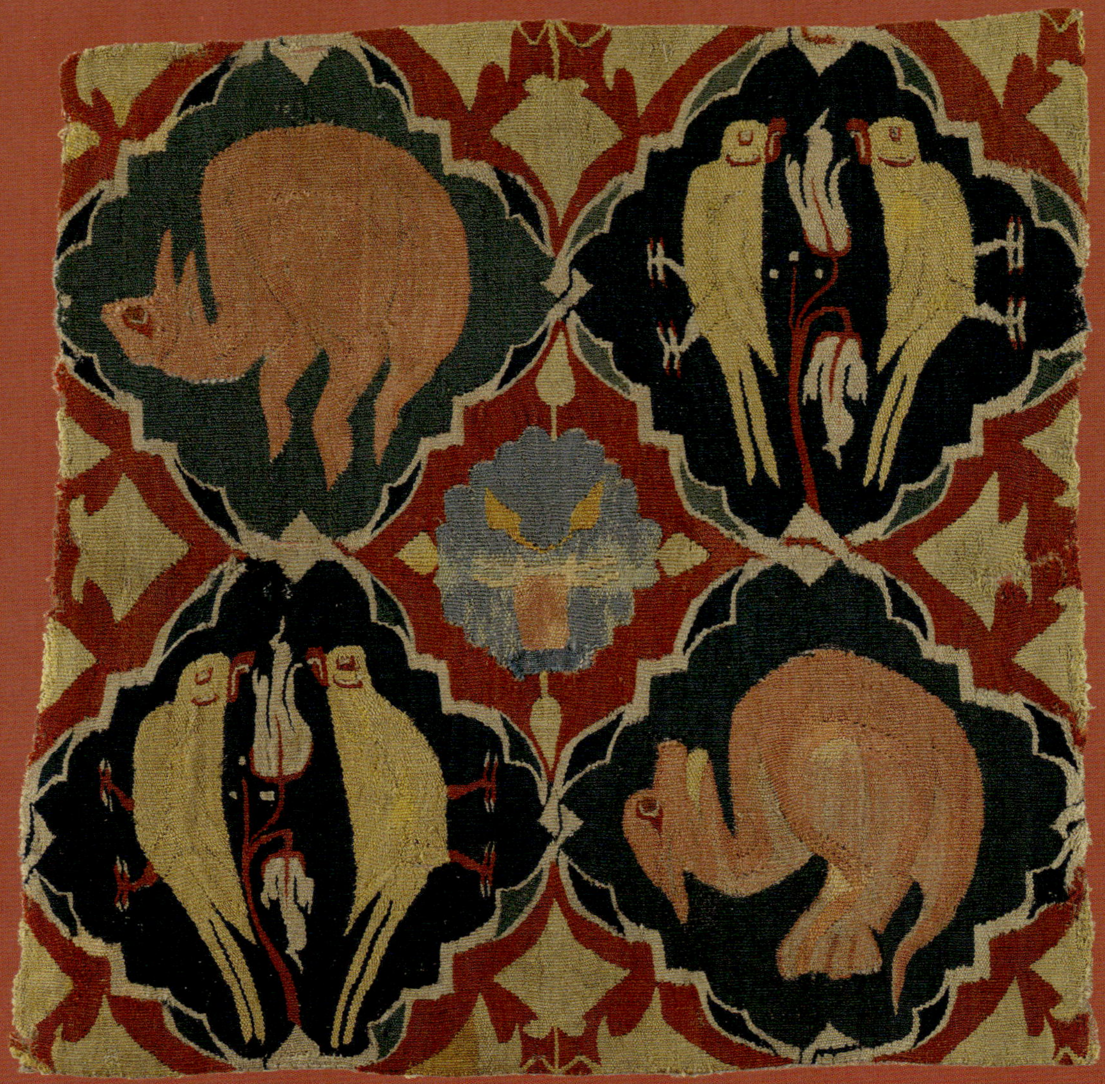

Fragment with Parrots and Dragons,
about 1300–50
Possibly made in Upper Rhine, Germany
Wool
56 cm x 56 cm
46.1

This small fragment is the oldest European tapestry purchased by Sir William Burrell. It is associated with a long tapestry woven with the same design from the Dominican Convent in Adelhausen, which is now in the Augustiner Museum in Freiburg im Breisgau, southwest Germany. Checked designs were popular during the Middle Ages and were produced not only on hangings, but also on wall and floor tiles. Parrots were associated with the Word of God, the Immaculate Conception of the Virgin Mary and Annunciation of Jesus Christ's birth. Here pairs of parrots are alternated with dragons, which symbolize the devil and evil.

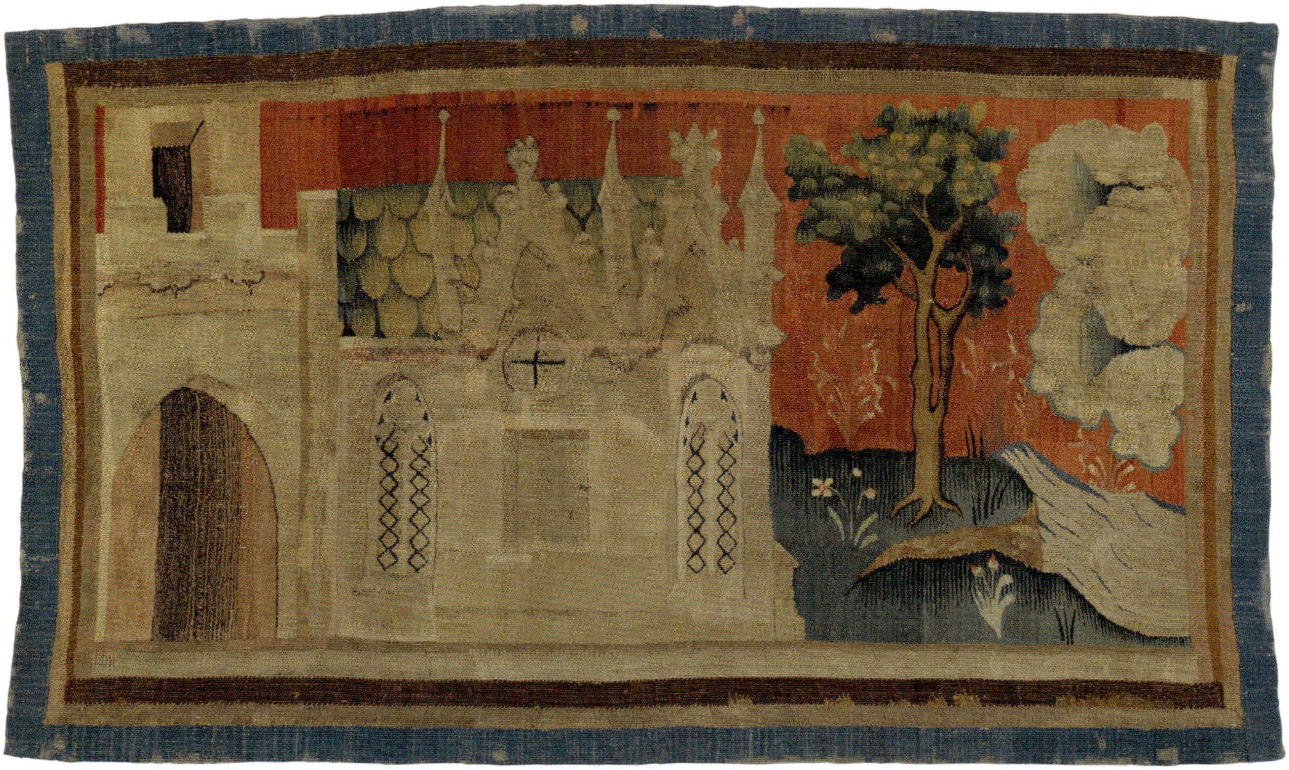

Church and Tree in a Landscape,

about 1373–80
Possibly made in the workshop of Robert Poinçon,
Paris, France
Wool
71 cm x 115 cm
46.54

The most famous and striking series of early medieval
tapestries are those depicting the Apocalypse, now in
Angers, France. This immense set was originally 140
metres long, from which the fragment of a *Church
and Tree* is believed to come from. The Angers
set was commissioned by Louis I, Duke of Anjou
(1339–84). Contemporary documents state that two
other series depicting the Apocalypse were made for
Louis's brothers, Jean, Duke of Berry (1340–1416)
and Philip the Bold, Duke of Burgundy (1342–1404).
Although the *Angel* was at first thought to be from
the Anjou tapestry, it is more likely to be a fragment
from one of the other two versions of the Apocalypse.

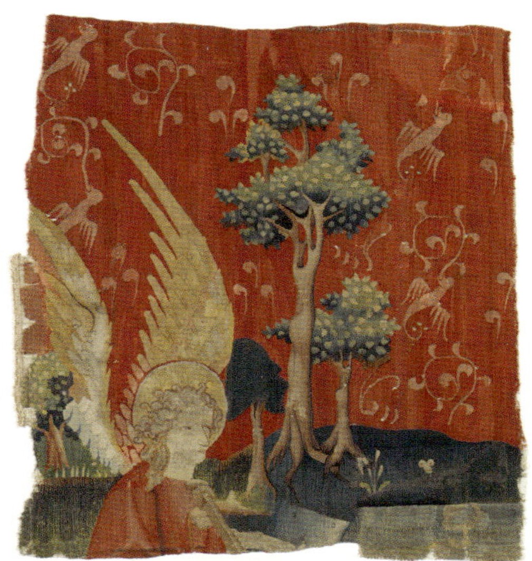

Angel in a Landscape, about 1386–1410

Possibly made in Paris, France
Wool
97 x 88 cm
46.53

Object in Focus

Armorial Tapestry of Beaufort, Turenne and Comminges, about 1350–95
Probably made in Paris or possibly Arras, France
Wool
224.5 cm x 224 cm
46.50

Coats of arms depicting a heraldic device on a shield or escutcheon were granted to individuals and their families as a sign of their importance and status. Armorial tapestries that incorporated these coats of arms were bespoke commissions made specifically for those who wanted to celebrate their family's connections.

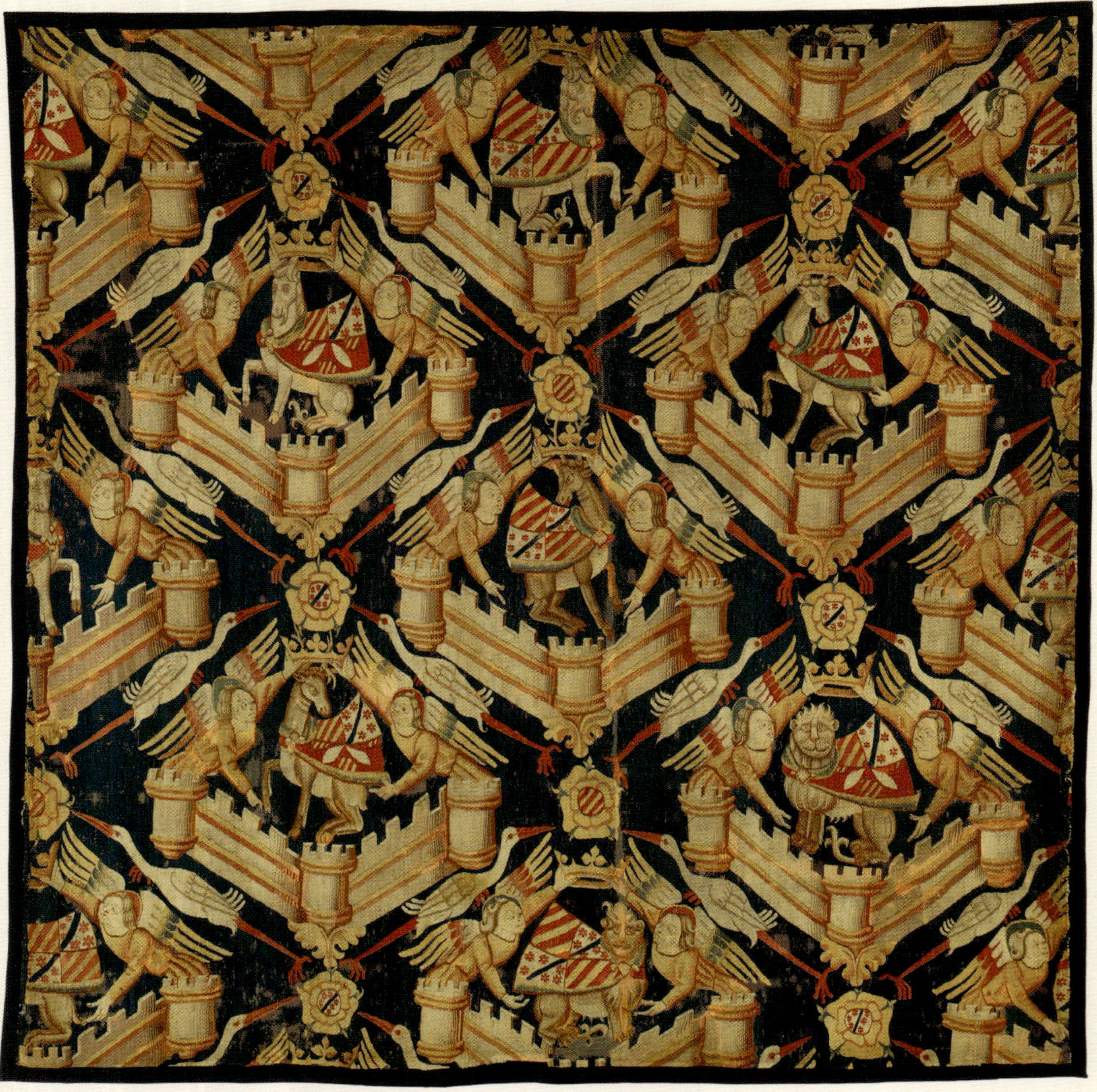

Each individual element of the design on this tapestry relates to the original owners, Guillaume III Rogier (1310–95), Count of Beaufort and Viscount of Turenne, and his wife, Aliénor de Comminges (d. 1397), who Rogier married in 1349. Their coats of arms are shown on the saddle-cloths worn by the deer, elephants, lions and unicorns. The diamond-shaped battlements play on the fam ly title of Beaufort, which translates as 'beautiful strong'. The storks stretched between them are the attribute of St Agricola of Avignon, the Papal state of which Rogier was Rector.

The storks' beaks point towards roses that symbolize the Rogier family's historic title of 'Lords of the Rose Gardens' in Rosiers d'Egletons, a town in central France.

Several of these armorials survive in museum collections across the world. Sir William Burrell was able to acquire three, each purchased individually, which he displayed in Hutton Castle, his home and country estate in the Scottish Borders.

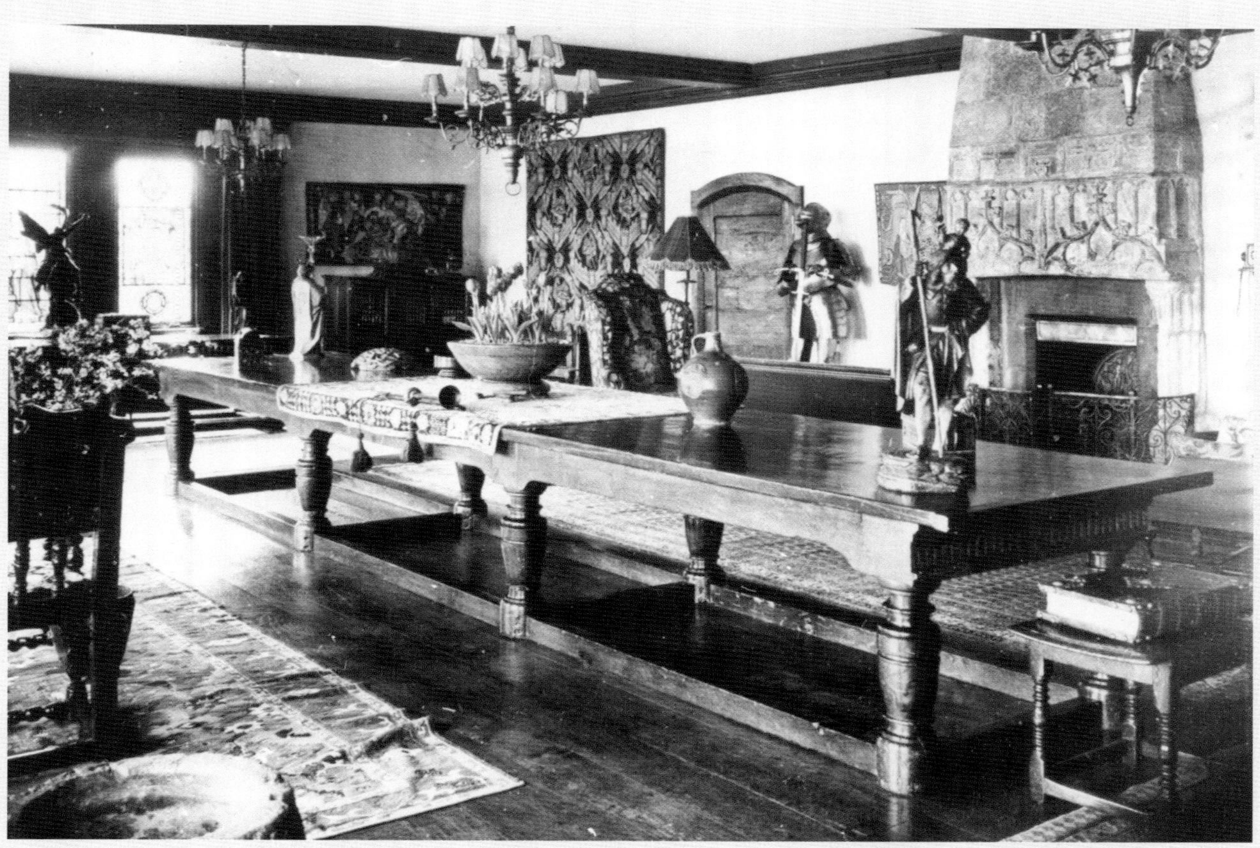

Armorial tapestry of Beaufort, Turenne and Comminges displayed by the Burrells in the Dining Room at Hutton Castle, Berwickshire. Glasgow Museums Archive, GMA.2013.1.1.499.

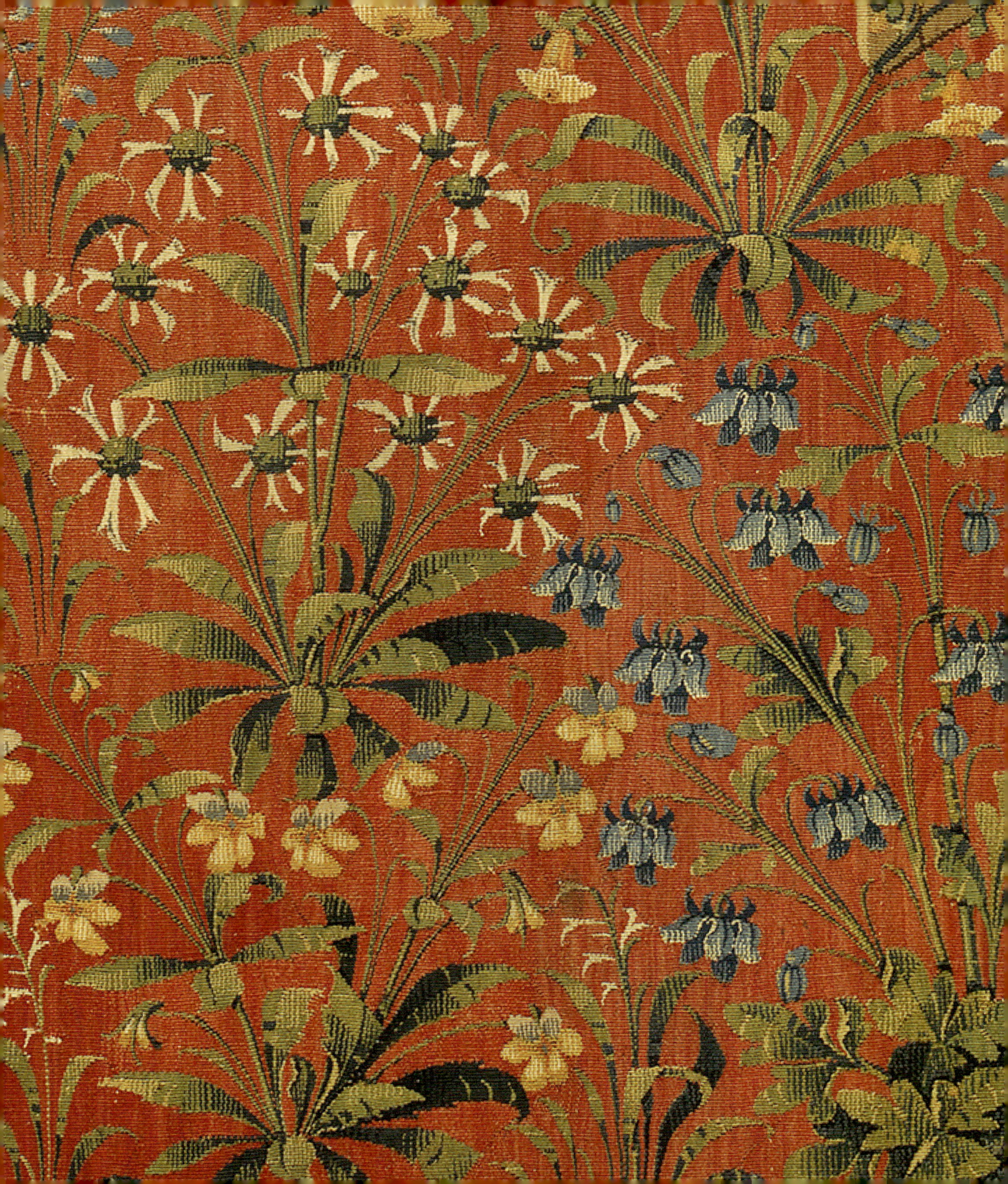

Fifteenth-century Tapestries

By the late medieval period tapestry workshops were well established. The largest and most prestigious were in the Southern Netherlands and northern France. Here, predominantly large-scale tapestries, often produced as a series of four to 12 scenes, were commissioned by the leading royal houses of Europe. Subject matters were diverse, ranging from classical myths and Biblical stories to allegories and secular scenes of hunting or seasonal labours.

Smaller workshops were also beginning to develop in German states, Switzerland and Alsace. These produced smaller-scale tapestries for churches rather than cathedrals, and for the newly emerging wealthy merchants, bankers and professionals, who sought to model their homes on those of the aristocratic classes, but had more limited means and wall space.

One of the most striking aspects of Sir William Burrell's collection of tapestries is that both the grand Southern Netherlandish tapestries as well as the more modest Swiss tapestries appealed to him. Burrell meticulously recorded all his purchases from 1911 onwards in a series of notebooks stating from where, when and for how much each item was bought. During the 1930s and 1940s several important collections came on the market, some as the result of forced sales during the Nazi Era (1933–45), but unlike today questions over provenance were not always asked or answered.

The majority of Burrell's tapestries were bought from dealers in Britain, Europe and the United States of America. The French dealer M & S Stora in Paris sold Burrell *The Boar Hunt* and *The Bear Hunt*. London-based Frank Partridge sold *Peasants Preparing to Hunt Rabbits with Ferrets*, which had been owned previously by the American newspaper magnate William Randolph Hearst. John Hunt (1900–76) was both a dealer and collector; *The Camel Caravan* had hung in his drawing room at Poyle Manor, Buckinghamshire, before he sold it to Burrell in 1937.

Opposite: Burrell's Purchase Book for 1938 notes this tapestry 'shows the typical millesfleurs decoration composed of flowers and leafwork of the most varied kind strewn against a rose ground' and was 'from the Collection of the Count of Charensay'. *Wild Man Guarding a Coat of Arms* (detail; see also p.38).

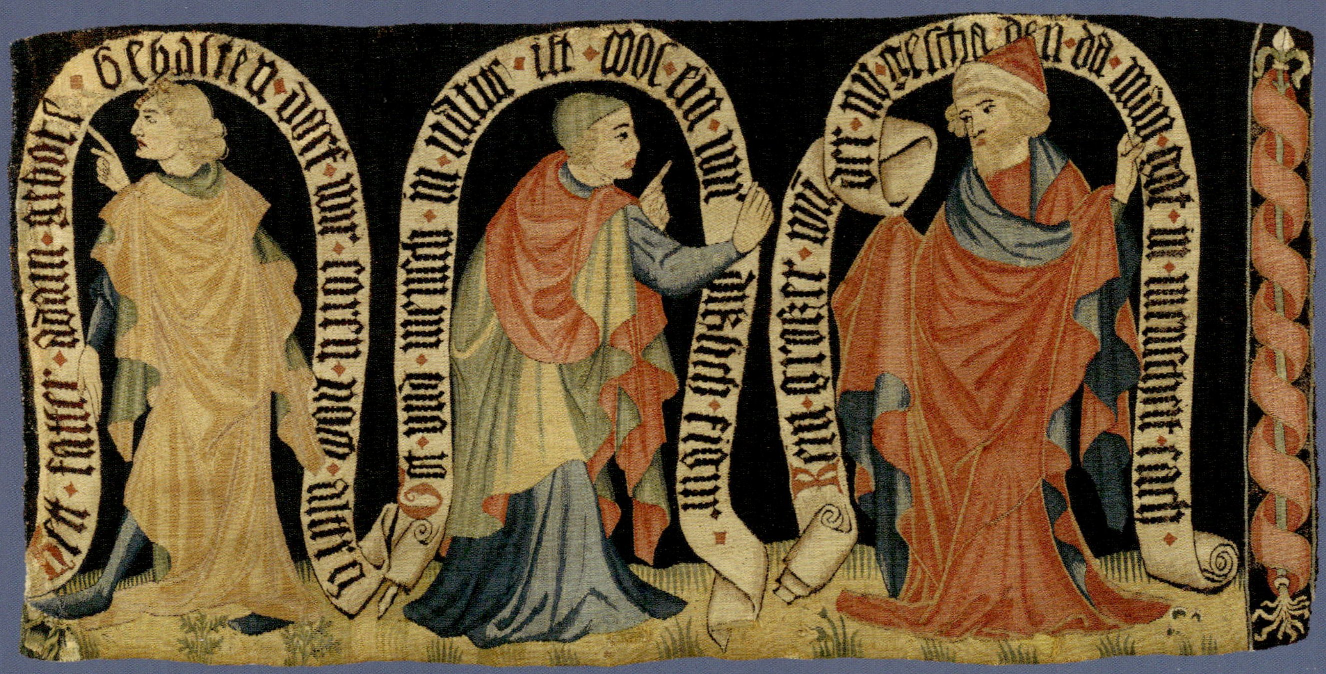

Three Prophets, about 1400–25
Made in Germany
Wool
63 cm x 127 cm
46.3

This fragment shows three men in long, flowing robes conversing, although the one on the left has lost his fellow speaker. The long scrolls or banderols arranged in arches over each figure contain their proverb-like phrases written in Franconian German; 'If father Adam would have obeyed the commandment, we would still be what we were', 'God and man in nature is certainly a true proposition' and 'No greater miracle ever happened than when man saw God in mankind'. A similar tapestry that shows a longer line of six pairs of figures is now in the Germanisches Nationalmuseum, Nuremberg.

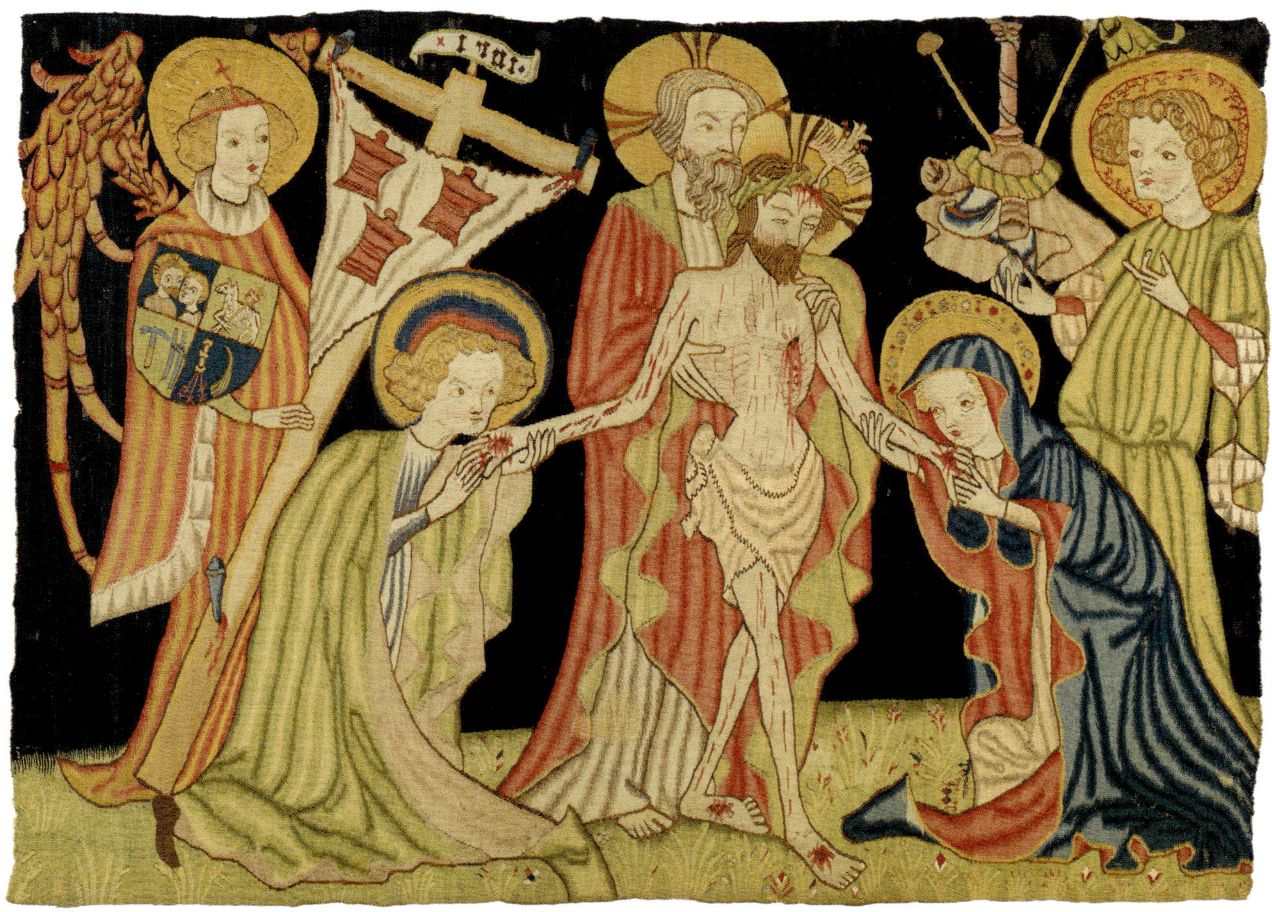

Holy Trinity with the Virgin, St John and Angels, about 1420

Made in Nuremberg, Bavaria, Germany
Wool, linen, silk
91 cm x 125 cm
46.10

The size of this fragment and the choice of religious subject suggest that this was probably used as part of an altar frontal or antependium. The Holy Trinity of Father, Son and Holy Spirit is shown in the centre with God supporting the resurrected Jesus Christ while the dove of the Holy Spirit flies in. The Angels either side hold symbols of Christ's Passion.

Burrell first attempted to buy this tapestry at a sale in 1928, but was outbid when it sold for £4,200. He finally bought it for £5,400 in 1945, which after 17 years' inflation was a relative bargain.

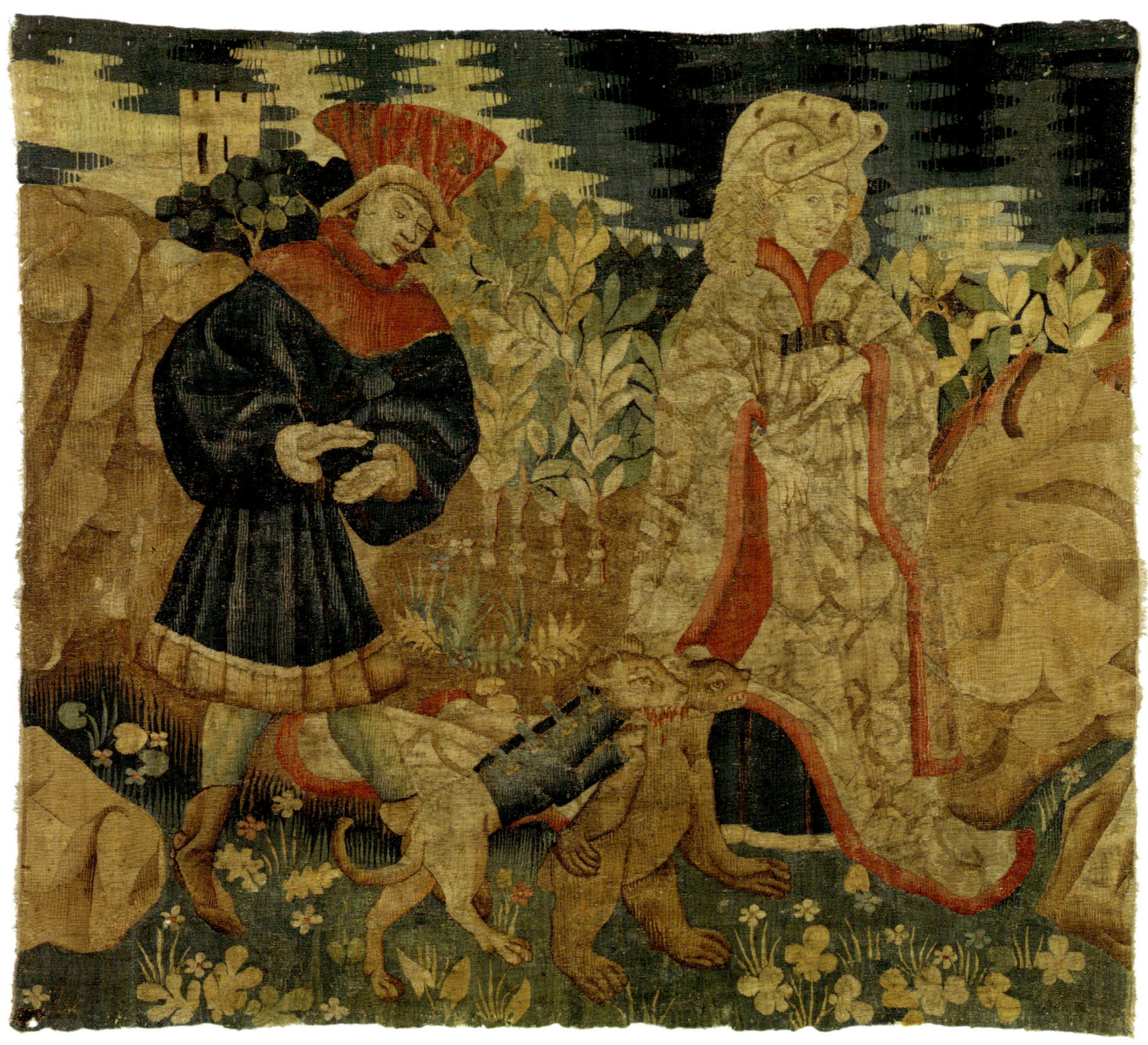

Bear Hunt, about 1435–40
Made in Southern Netherlands, now Belgium
Wool, metal thread
163 cm x 177 cm
46.62

Hunting was a popular secular topic for tapestries, particularly those made for sale to wealthy, noble households. Many of those woven in the 1400s were traditionally attributed to Arras, France, where dealers including Jean Walois (fl.1411–45) are documented as selling large-scale tapestries depicting hunting scenes. However, many were woven in workshops in Tournai and Brussels, in the Southern Netherlands. These two fragments with their well-dressed noble gentlemen, ladies and attendants hunting a variety of different prey animals or quarries are stylistically similar to the much larger Devonshire Hunting Tapestries, now in the Victoria and Albert Museum, London.

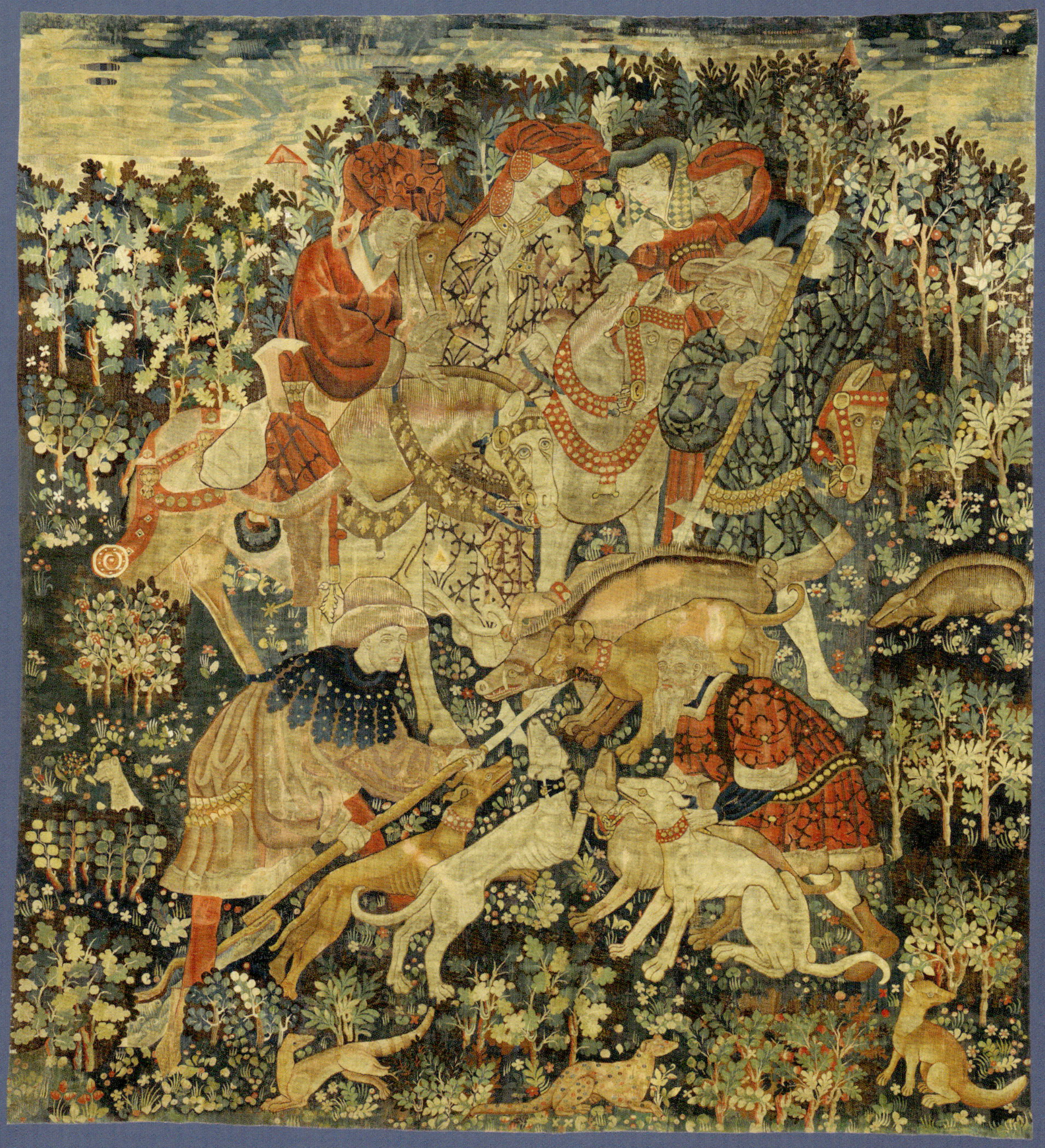

Boar Hunt, about 1435–50
Made in Southern Netherlands, now Belgium
Wool
409 cm x 363 cm
46.57

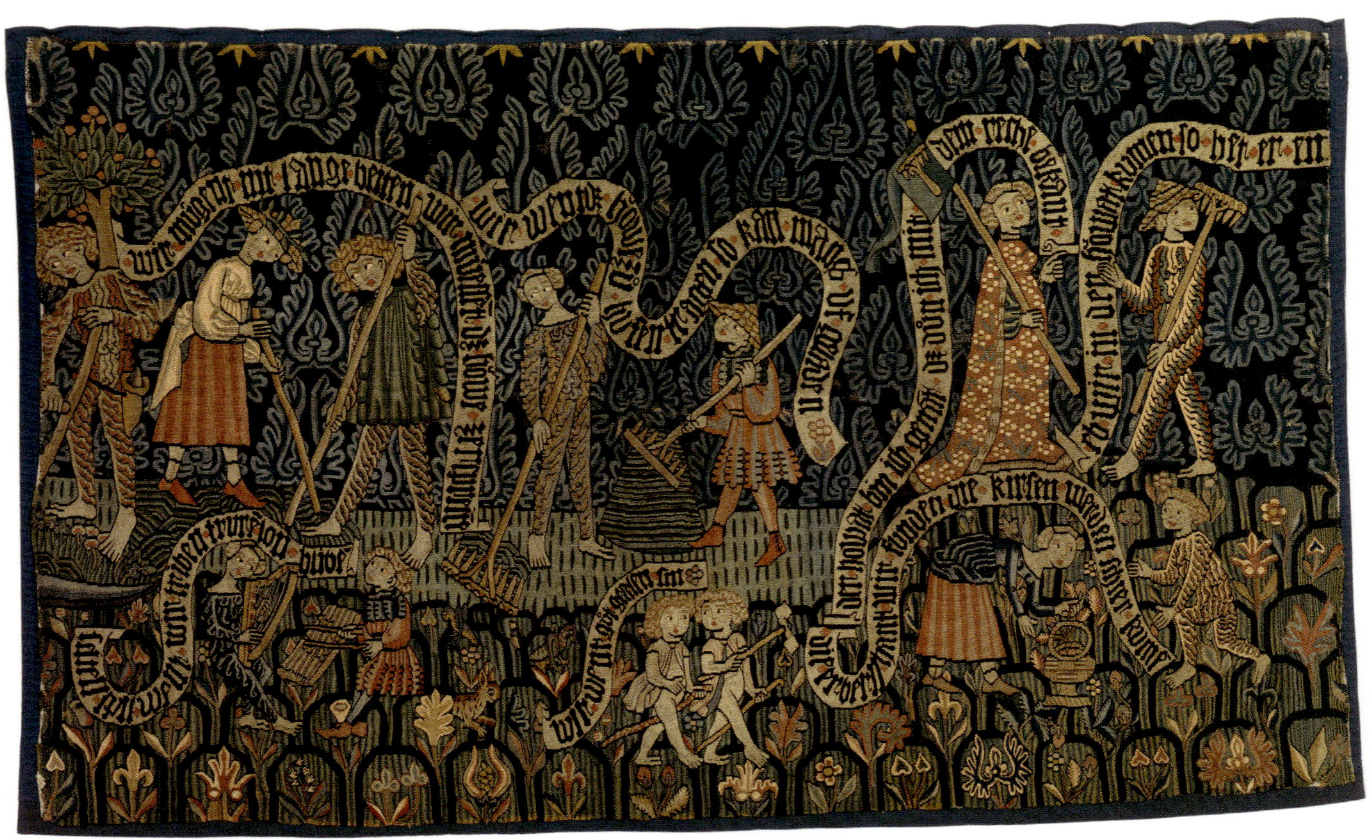

The Months: July – Haymaking, about 1440

Made in Alsace
Wool, linen
99 cm x 161 cm
46.26

Wild men and women appear in several tapestries woven in Alsace and Switzerland during the 1400s. In some they attack castles, in others they are being tamed, but here wild men and women are shown as good companions working alongside a noble woman and villagers. The scene symbolizes harmony between humankind and nature, the civilized and the untamed. The scrolls or banderols explain the tasks involved with the haymaking; 'we must spread the hay' and 'we will put the hay in heaps so that it can be loaded'. Bottom right the workers remark that 'we have found the strawberries; the cherries will be coming soon.'

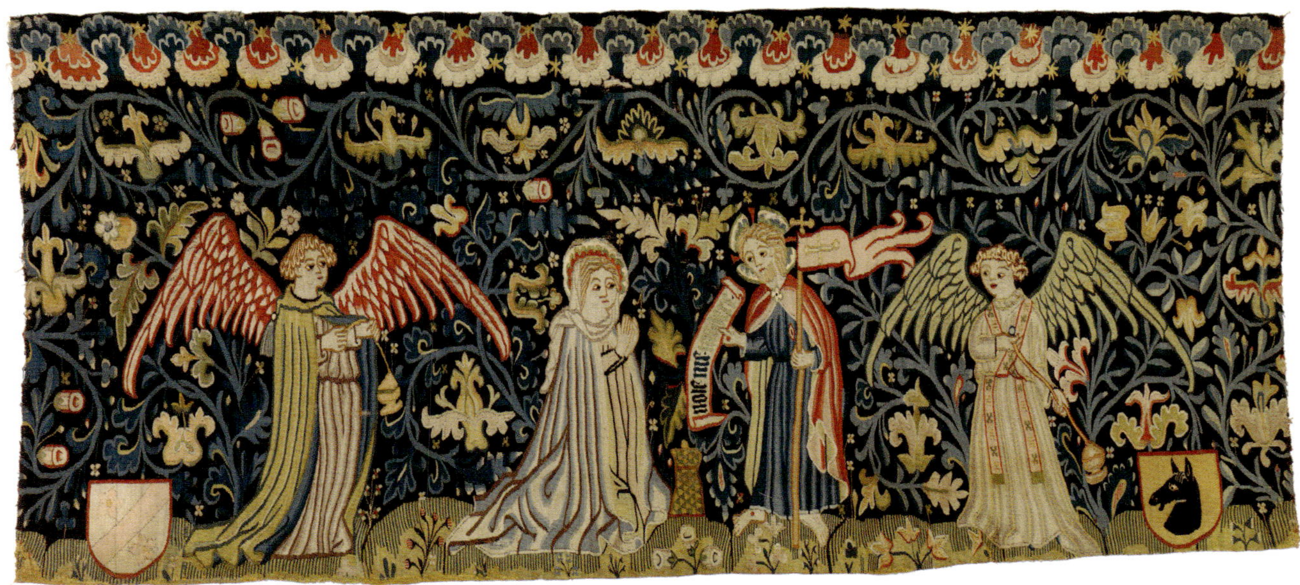

Noli me Tangere, about 1440–50
Made in Switzerland
Linen, wool, silk
92 cm x 205 cm
46.34

Here Mary Magdalene kneels before the resurrected Jesus Christ in a red cloak, his warning inscribed on the scroll 'Nole (sic) Me Tangere' ('Don't touch me'). The scene is taken from the Gospel of St John, where the full text reads 'Touch me not; for I am not yet ascended to my Father'.

The coats of arms of the Krauchthals of Berne and Von Velschens of Thun suggest that the donor of this tapestry was Petermann von Krauchthal (d.1425) or possibly his wife Anna von Velschen (d.1459), who as a widow became a patron of several religious institutions.

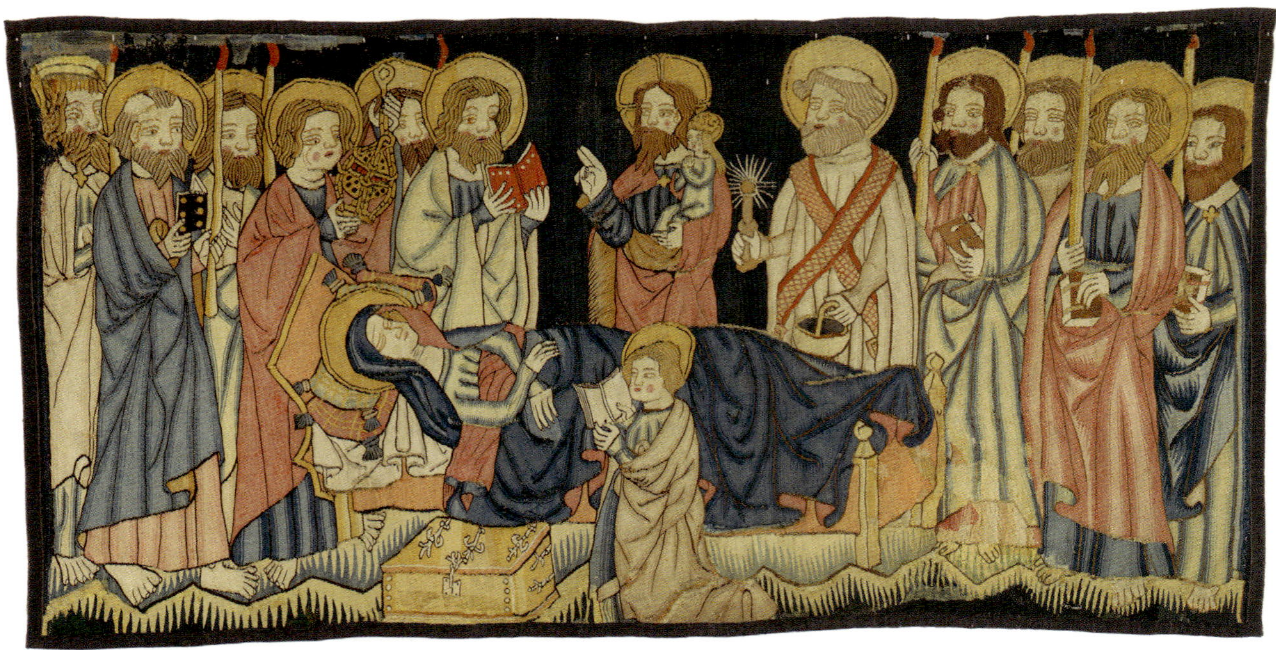

Death of the Virgin, about 1450
Made in Middle Rhine, Germany
Wool, linen
82 cm x 159 cm
46.17

The scene on this altar frontal is inspired by a collection of saints' lives compiled by Jacobus de Voragine, _The Golden Legend_, about 1260. The Virgin Mary, who is shown wearing her traditional blue mantle symbolizing purity, lies in the centre with Jesus Christ above. He holds a crowned child to represent the acceptance of Mary's soul into heaven. They are surrounded by the Twelve Apostles, who administer the last rites. On the left St John blows out an incense burner as a sign that a life has ended and on the right St Peter holds a sprinkler of holy water.

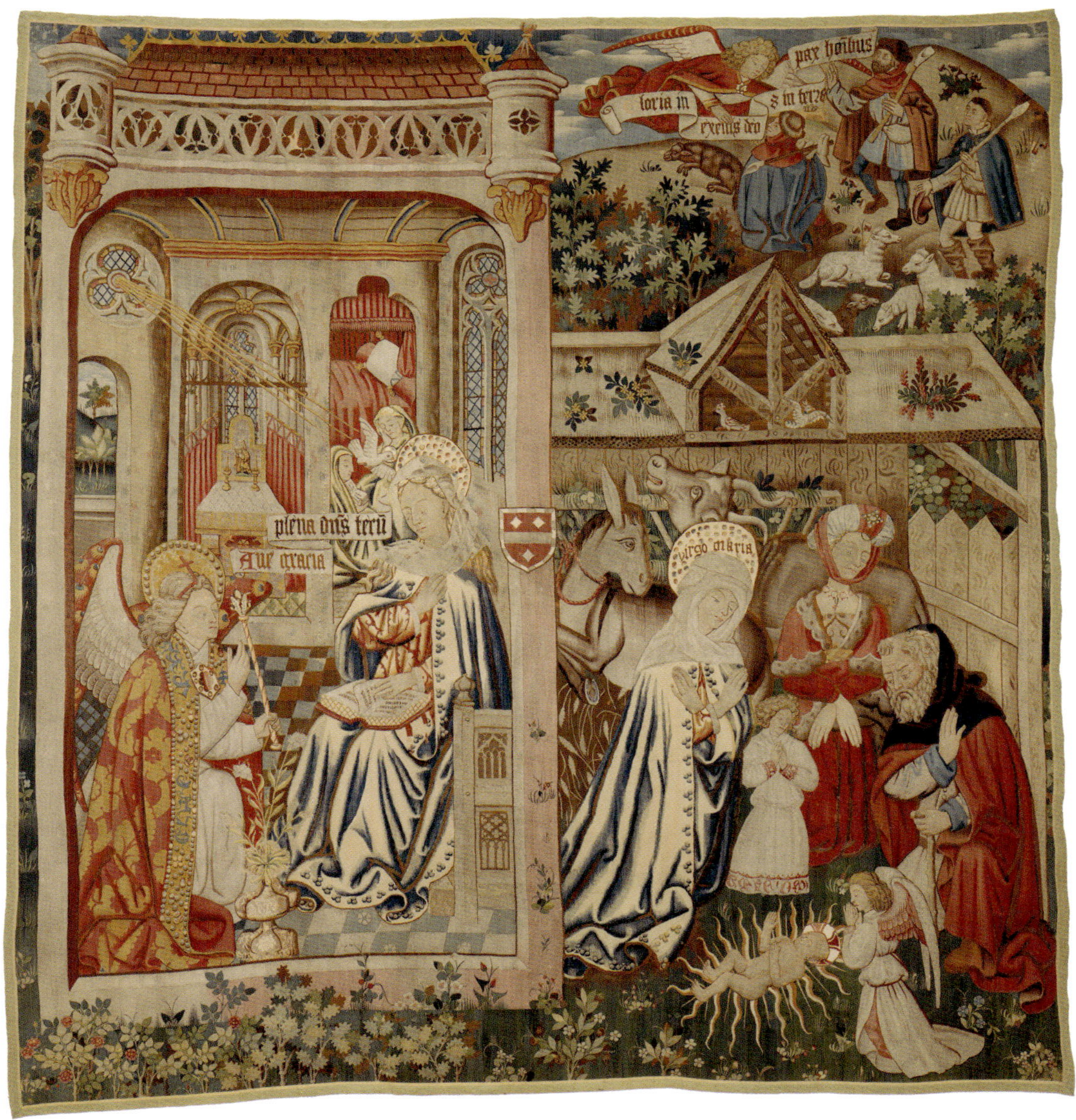

Annunciation and Nativity, about 1450
Made in Southern Netherlands, now Belgium
Wool, silk
480 cm x 452 cm
46.115

This beautifully-composed tapestry depicts
two scenes. On the left the Archangel Gabriel
kneels before the Virgin Mary with the rays
shining through the trefoil window indicating the
Holy Spirit. On the right the Nativity scene shows
the birth of Jesus including the midwife Salome
dressed in red. The style of the design is
reminiscent of Robert Campin (about 1375–1444)
and his leading apprentice, Rogier van der Weyden
(1399/1400–64). However, it is more likely the
cartoon was drawn by another apprentice,
Jacques Daret (about 1404–about 1470).

23

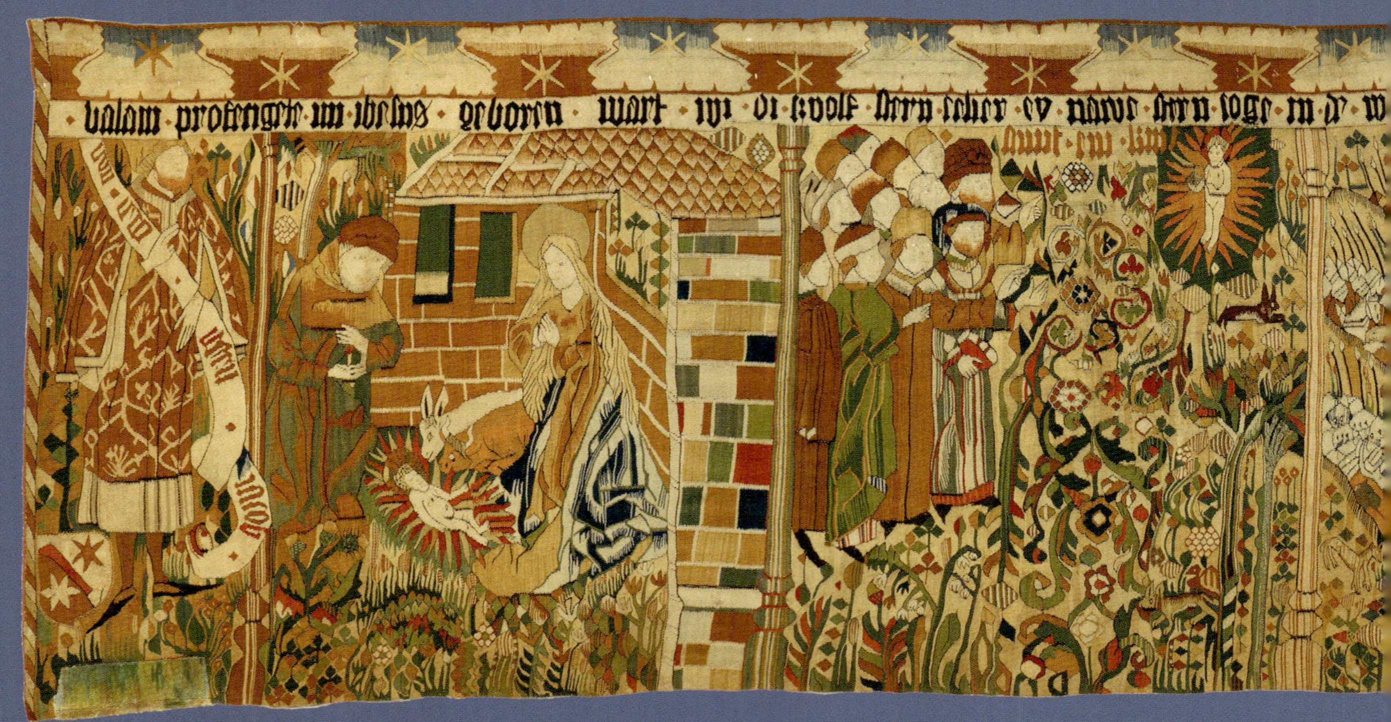

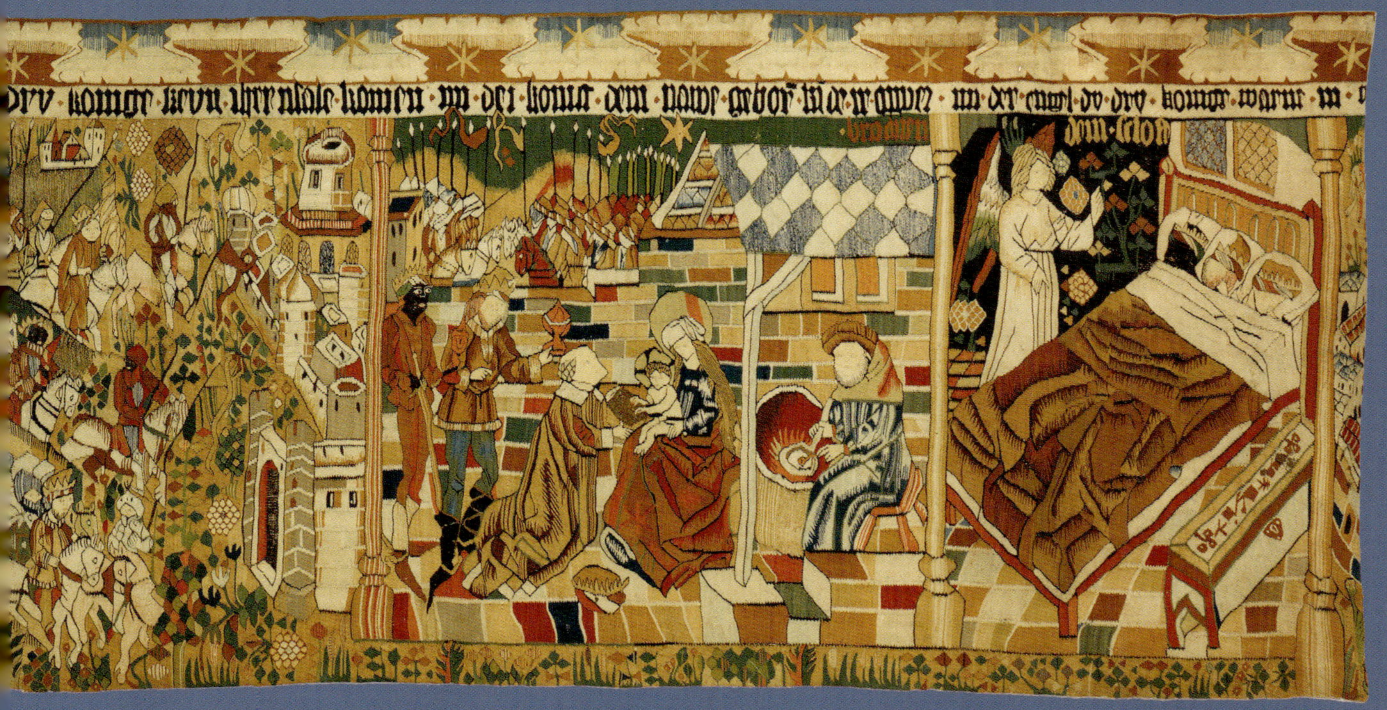

The Prophet Balaam and the Story of the Magi, abcut 1450–75

Made in Germany
Linen, woo!, metal, silk
110 cm x 393 cm
46.12

The inscription along the top of this long tapestry outlines the subject of the scenes below, including; 'Prophet Balam', who foretold the arrival of Christ, 'How Jesus was born', 'How the three magi came to Jerusalem', and 'How the Angel warns the magi in their sleep'.

By the early 1400s the Magi were often depicted in European art as not only representing three ages of man, but also the three known continents, Europe, Asia and Africa, with the latter represented by a black African. This may have stemmed from the description of Balthasar, the youngest Magi, by St Bede (about 673–735) as having a 'black complexion'.

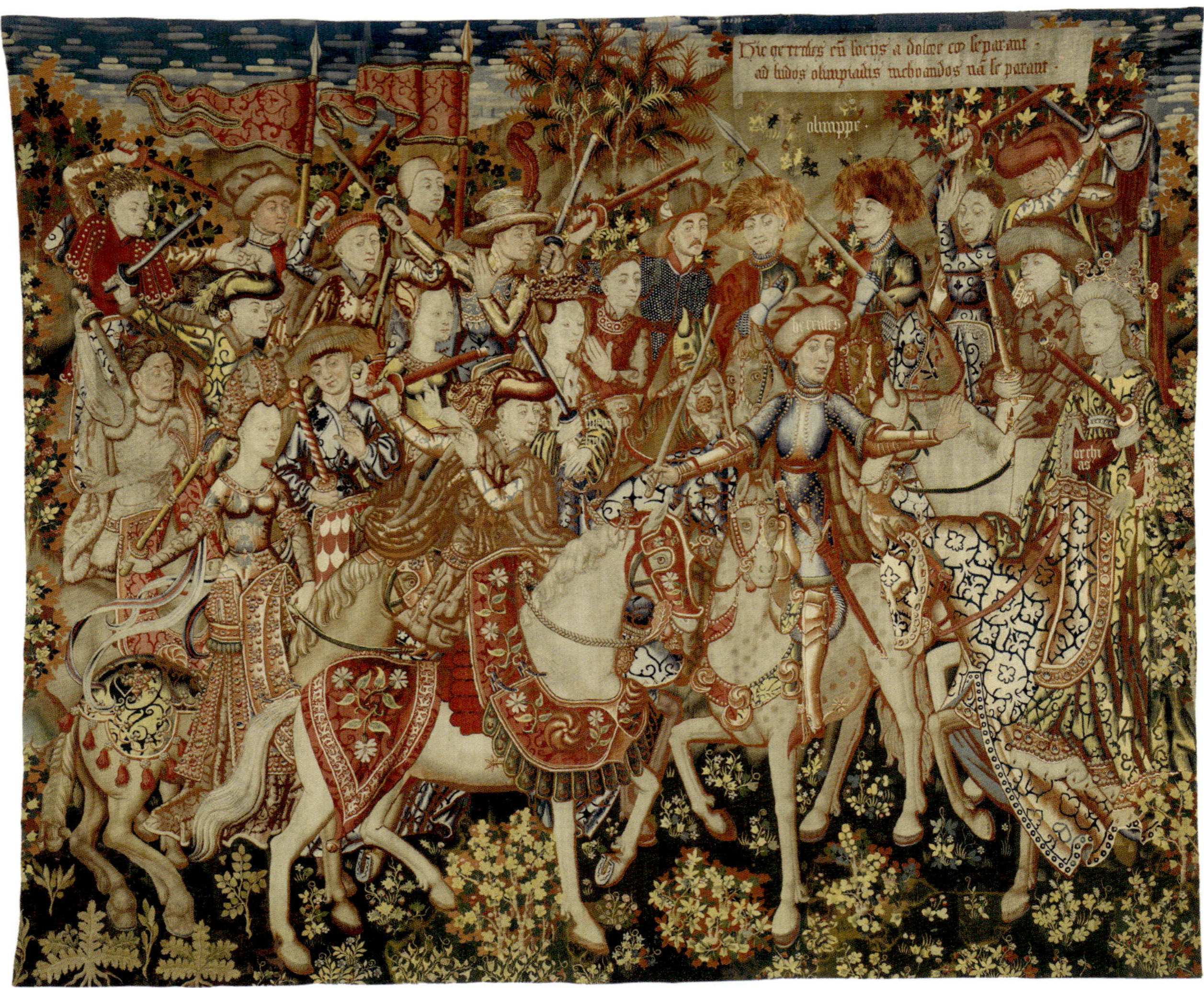

Hercules Founding the Olympic Games on Mount Olympus, about 1450

Made in Southern Netherlands, now Belgium
Wool, silk
409 cm x 484 cm
46.80

In medieval retellings of the legend of Hercules the hero's sixth labour was a tournament in which he and Theseus competed against the Amazon queen, Orithyia, and her daughters or sisters, Menalippe and Hippolyta. The scroll at the top explains what happens next; 'Here Hercules and his companions separate with sad heart, in order to prepare themselves for the Olympic games now beginning.'

In this stunning tapestry the Greek heroes and heroines do not wear classical dress, but instead wear the fashionable clothing worn at the most celebrated court in Europe, that of Philip the Good, Duke of Burgundy (1396–1467).

The Story of Troy was the subject of a series of 11 tapestries designed by the Coëtivy Master. At least nine different editions were made for the leading rulers in Europe, including Charles the Bold, Duke of Burgundy (1433–77), Henry VII of England (1457–1509) and James IV of Scots (1473–1513). This fragment is from the seventh tapestry and shows the embalmed body of Hector, Prince of Troy, being commemorated by his parents, King Priam and Queen Hecuba, his widow, Andromache, and the Trojans. The red banderol below is a fragment from the sixth tapestry in the series and tells of an earlier battle when Achilles killed the giant, Hupon the Great.

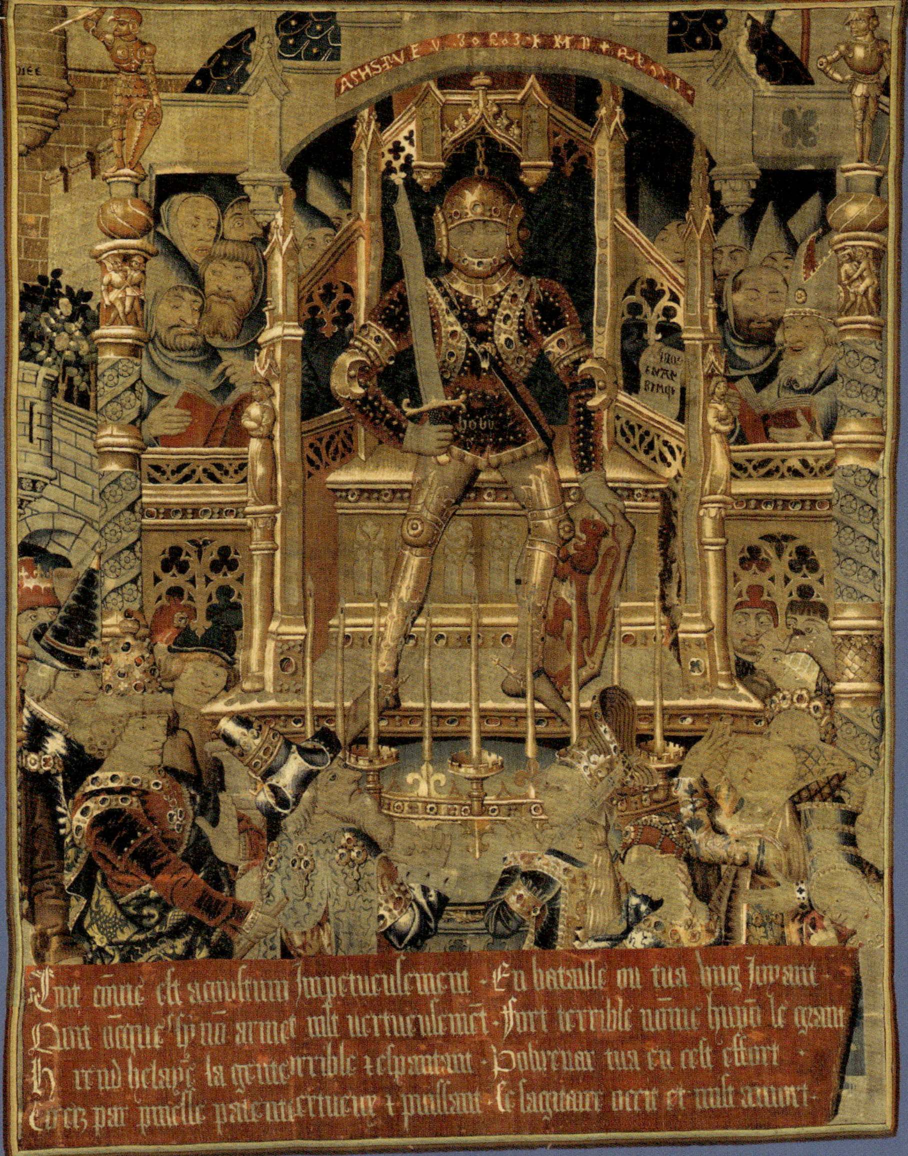

The Story of Troy: Hector's Tomb upon the Anniversary of his Death, about 1465–95
Designed by the Coëtivy Master, made in Southern Netherlands, now Belgium
Wool, silk
357 cm x 270 cm
46.83

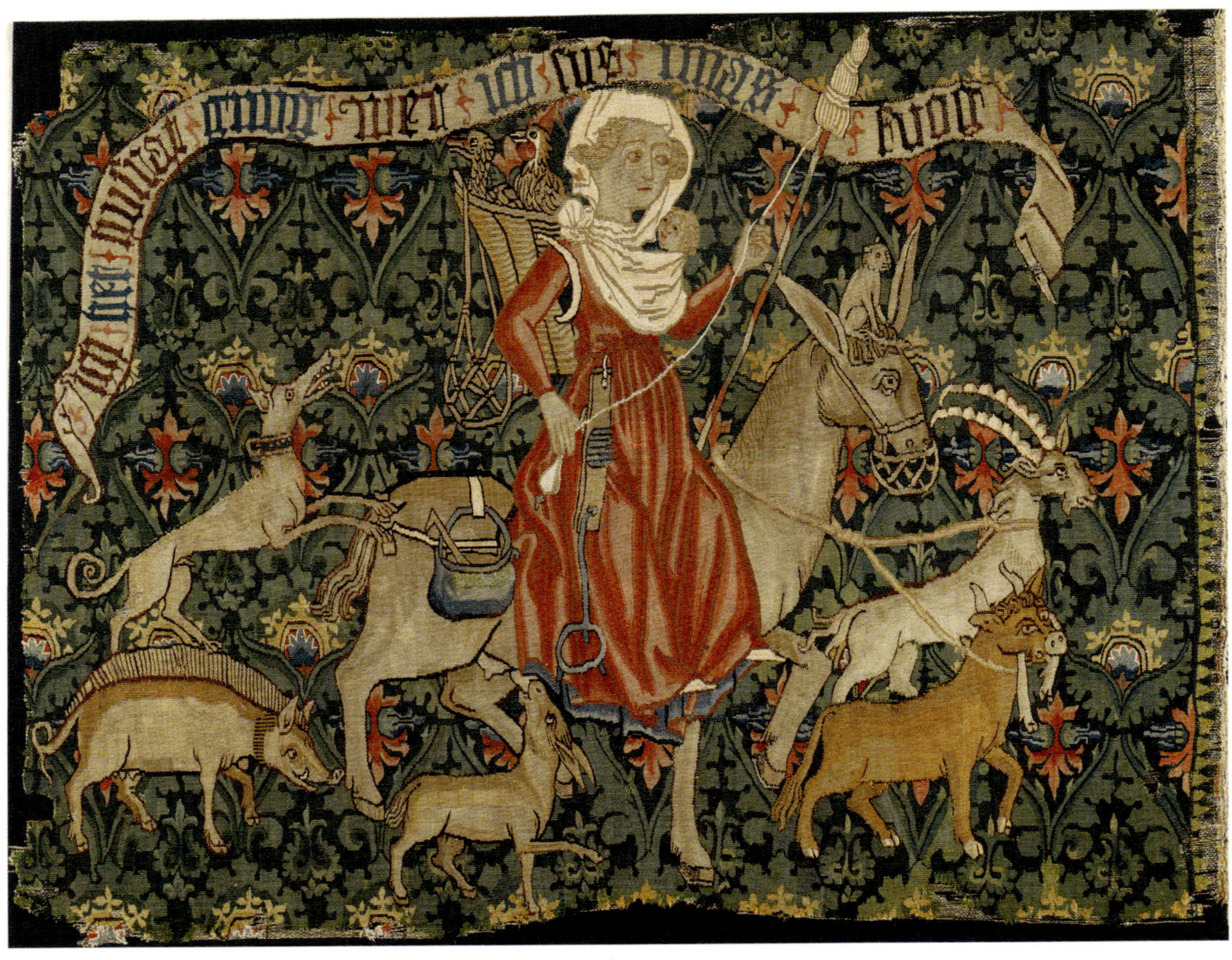

The Wandering Housewife, about 1470–80
Made in Switzerland
Wool, linen, metal threads
86 cm x 109 cm
46.39

The scroll on this tapestry states 'I have plenty of household goods; otherwise I would not be so important'. The wandering housewife's possessions include a distaff for spinning, a pot for cooking and two ducks, a dog, boards, goats and the donkey on which she and her baby ride. Today it is not clear how to interpret this tapestry – is she being singled out for praise for her ability to multi-task or being criticized for being over-busy? Another slightly larger tapestry showing this scene now in the Museum of Applied Art, Cologne, includes a man being shooed away. Is she too busy even for love or pleasure?

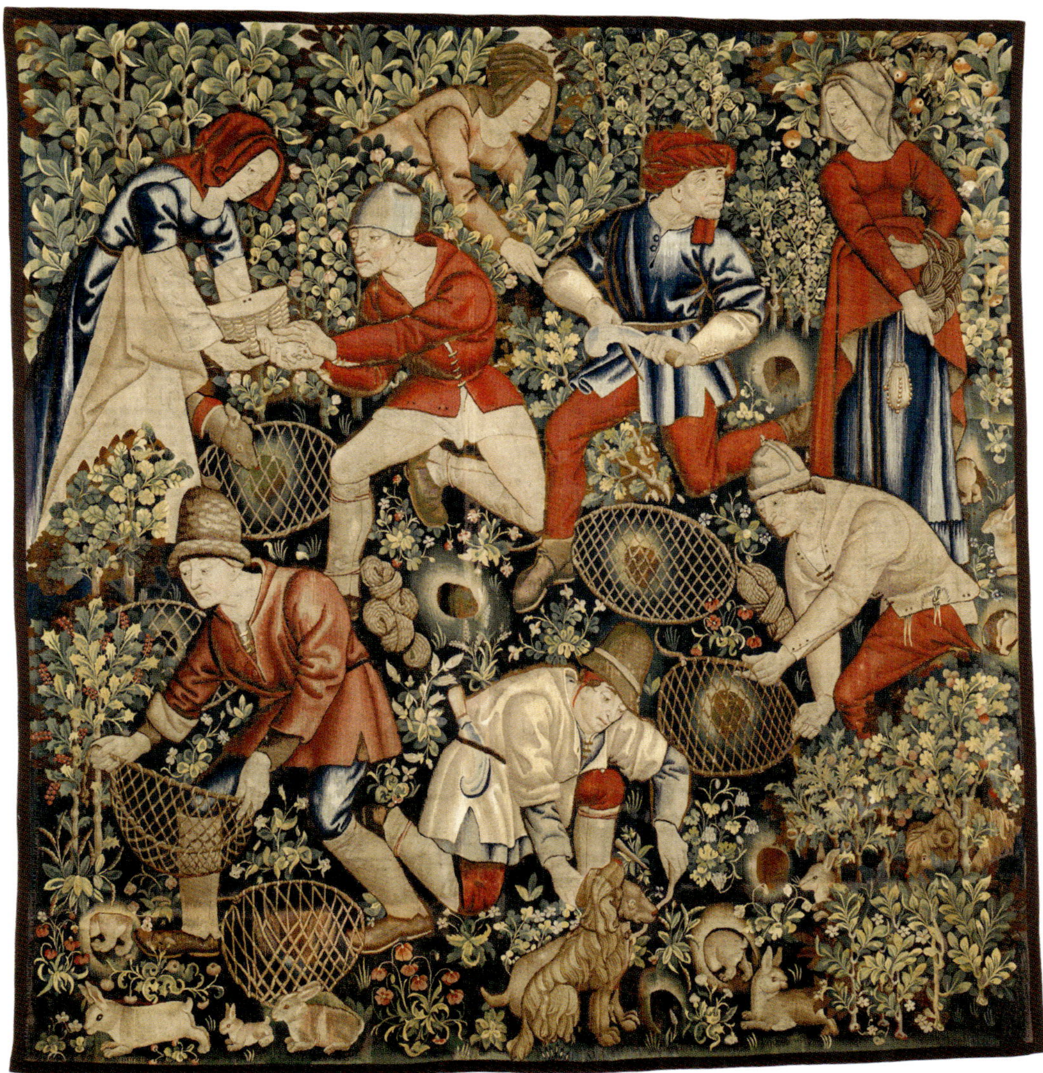

Peasants Preparing to Hunt Rabbits with Ferrets, about 1470–90

Possibly made in Brussels, Brabant, Southern Netherlands, now Belgium
Wool, silk
323 cm x 300 cm
46.56

In this first scene of a series of tapestries showing The Rabbit Hunt the relatively well-dressed peasants are preparing to hunt. They place purse nets at the exits of rabbit burrows, and then release a trained ferret from a basket to chase the rabbits out. This method of hunting was popular during the Middle Ages, and was described in contemporary manuals, such as Gaston III, Count of Foix, *Livre de Chasse*, 1387–89. The other tapestries showing *The Hunt Underway* and *The Peasant's Picnic* are now in the Fine Arts Museums of San Francisco and the Louvre Museum, Paris.

Object in Focus

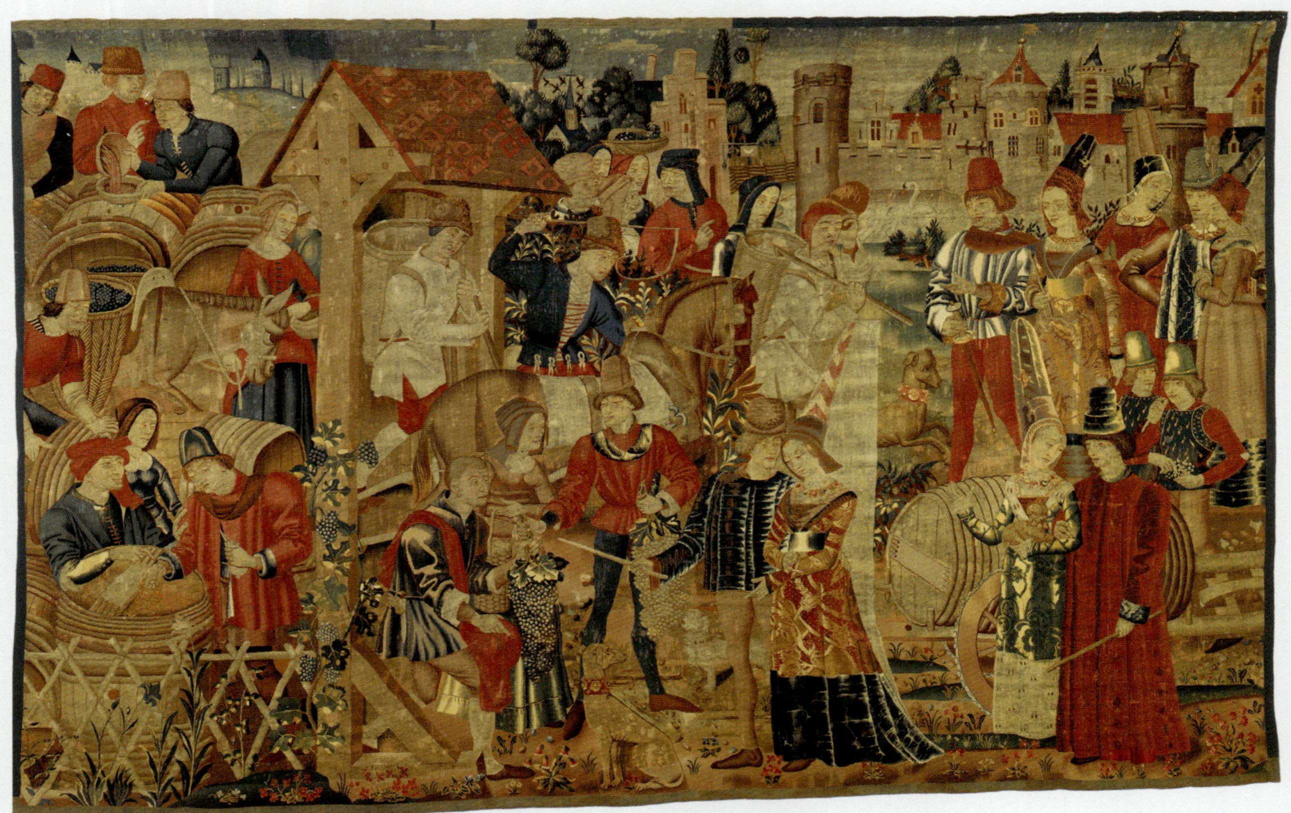

Scenes of Wine Making: Distribution of the Vintage, about 1475
Design attributed to Dieric Bouts or a follower, probably made in Brussels, Brabant, Southern Netherlands, now Belgium
Wool, silk
345 cm x 539 cm
46.68

Opposite: *Dining Room at 8 Great Western Terrace,* 1902, by R Miliken. Glasgow Museums Archive, 52.40.1.1.

At the centre top of this busy scene grape harvesters bring in the fruit from the field. On the left workers draw wine samples for checking while on the right aristocratic couples wearing contemporary Burgundian fashions are shown the quality of the grapes in expectation of them buying the wine.

This was the most expensive tapestry bought by William Burrell, purchased on 3 June 1927 for £12,600. It is part of a large series of tapestries showing *Scenes of Wine Making* from the grapes being tended on the vine through to the sale of the vintage. Only a few pieces remain, including *Vintners in a Wine Press*, which was one of the first tapestries acquired by Burrell. He incorporated it into the furnishing of the Dining Room at his and Constance's first home at 8 Great Western Terrace, Glasgow.

Distribution of the Vintage depicts the previous scene in the series. A wealthy man, featured bottom right, is shown the process of making wine. Wine-makers, or vinters, work to press grapes in the large mechanical press in the centre. From there the juice flows into a large vat, where it is blessed before being decanted into barrels.

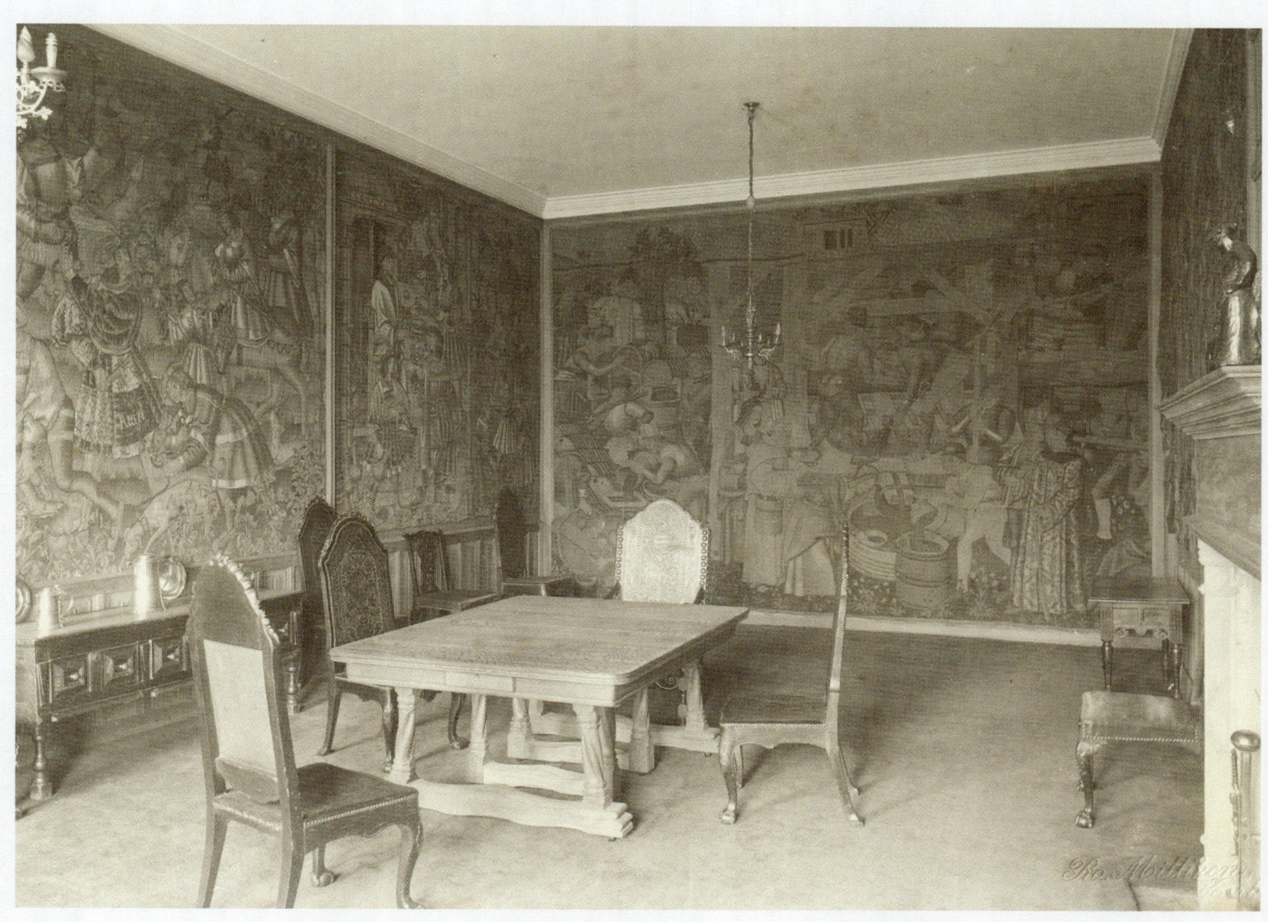

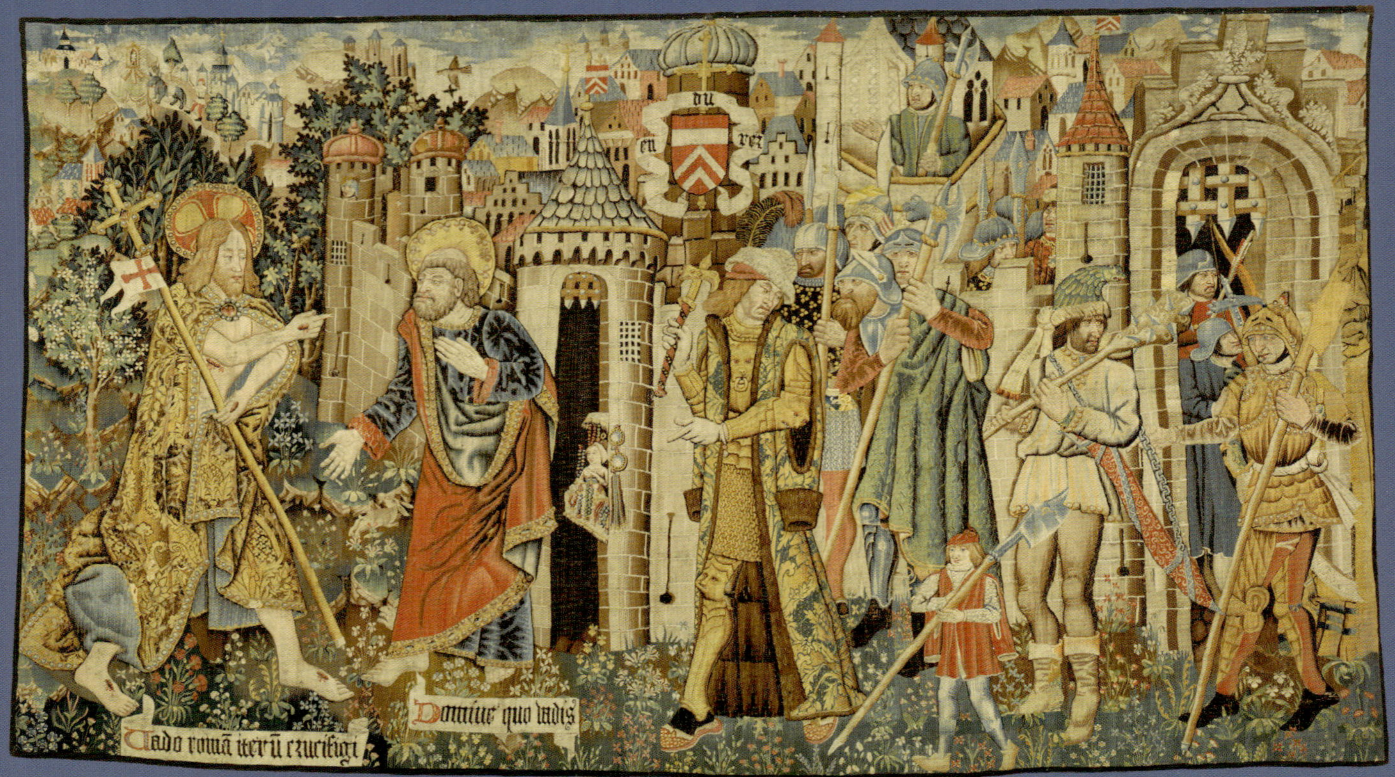

**Scenes from the Life of Saint Peter:
'Quo Vadis',** about 1475
Made in Southern Netherlands, now Belgium
Wool
286 cm x 506 cm
46.123

This tapestry is from a series of seven depicting Scenes from the Life of St Peter commissioned by Antoine de Poisieu (d. 1496), Abbot of the Benedictine abbey of St Peter in Vienna. On the left Peter, who has just left Rome, meets the resurrected Jesus Christ and asks him *'Domine, quo vadis'* ('Master, where are you going?'). Christ replies *'Vado roma iteru crucifigi'* ('I am going to Rome to be crucified again'), prompting Peter to return to Rome, where he will be met by the soldiers of the provost Agrippa, who gather on the right of this tapestry, and sentenced to death for his faith.

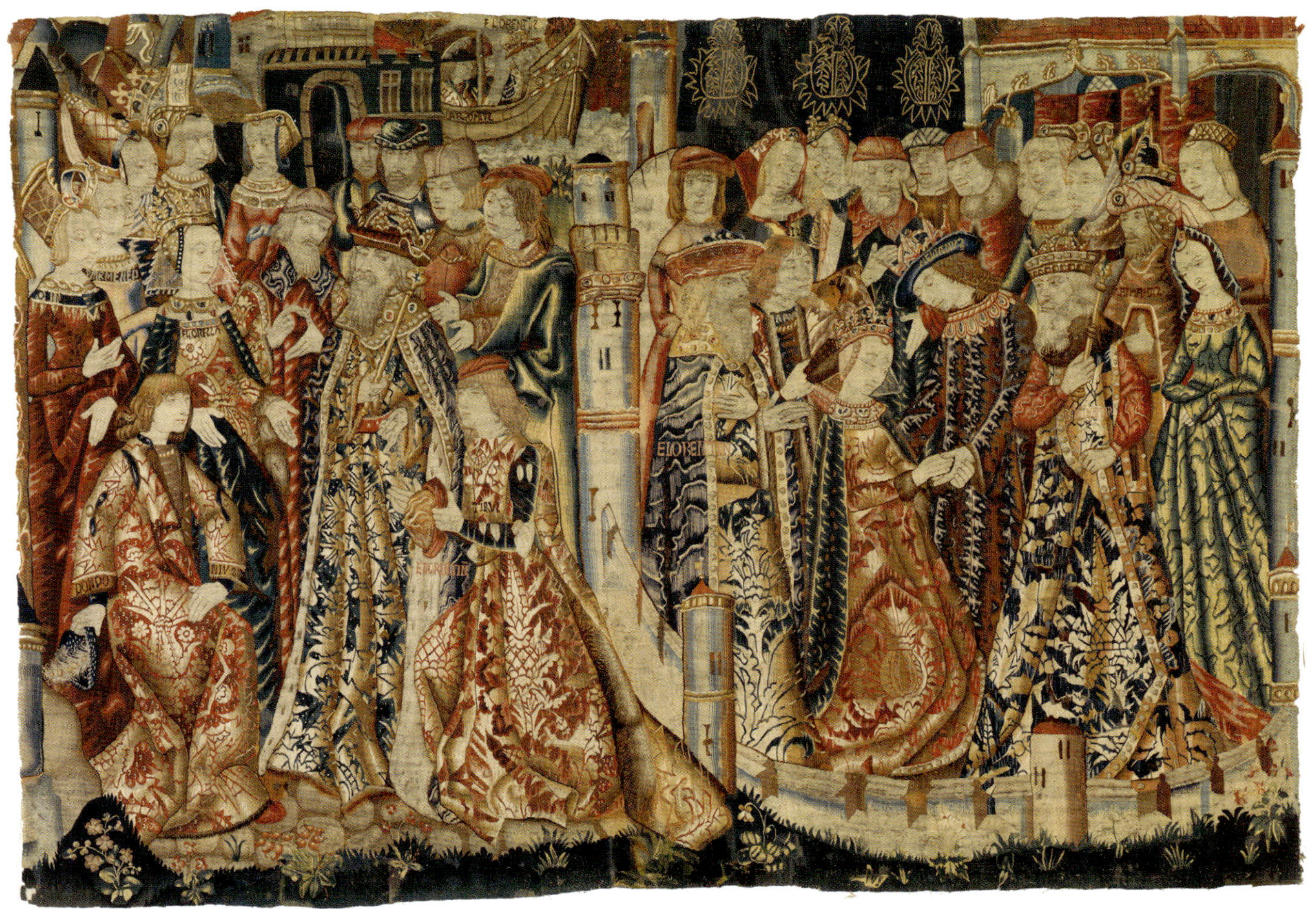

Two Episodes from a Chivalric Romance, perhaps the tale of Florence of Rome,
about 1480
Possibly made in Brussels, Southern Netherlands, now Belgium
Wool, silk
210 cm x 301 cm
46.93

The tale shown in this fabulous tapestry is not clear today. One possibility is that it depicts Florence, Empress of Rome, whose tale was told in Christine of Pisan's (1360–1431), *Book of the City of Ladies*, 1405. Florence was slandered by her brother-in-law after he failed to seduce her. Her husband, the Emperor, subsequently sentenced her to death. Florence fled and endured further troubles before a vision of the Virgin Mary directed her to a herb that allowed her to extract confessions from her false accusers, leading to her vindication.

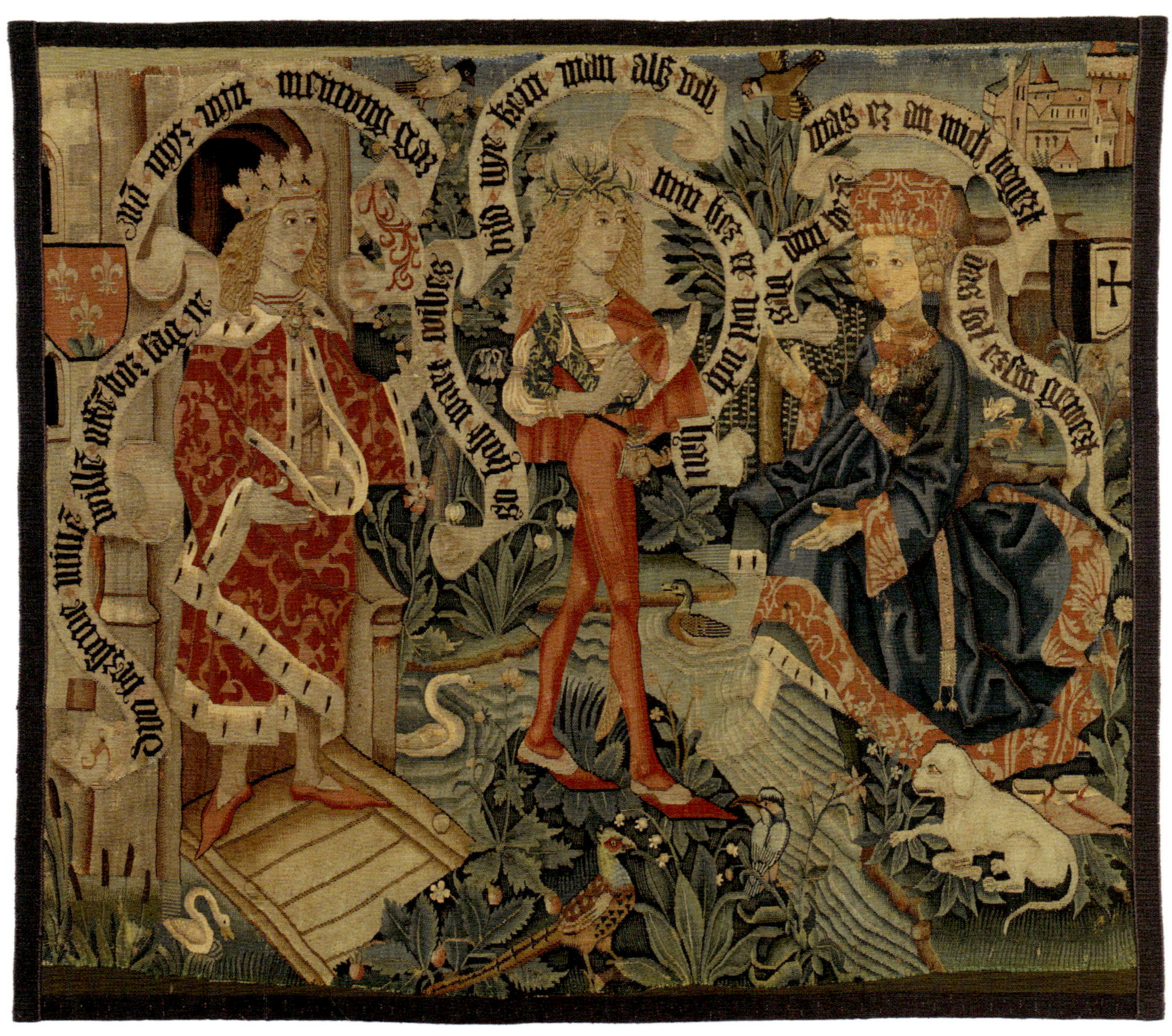

David and Bathsheba, about 1480
Made in Alsace
Wool, linen, silk, metal thread
93 cm x 104 cm
46.27

The banderols or scrolls in this colourful tapestry narrate the exchange between King David and the beautiful Bathsheba, wife of one of his generals, communicated through the young page carrying a love letter in the centre. David has instructed the page to 'Reveal to her my will; tell her of my intention'. The page subsequently gushes to Bathsheba 'There never was a man so in love as my master; he wants to possess you' to which she replies 'Tell your master, what he wishes from me shall be granted'.

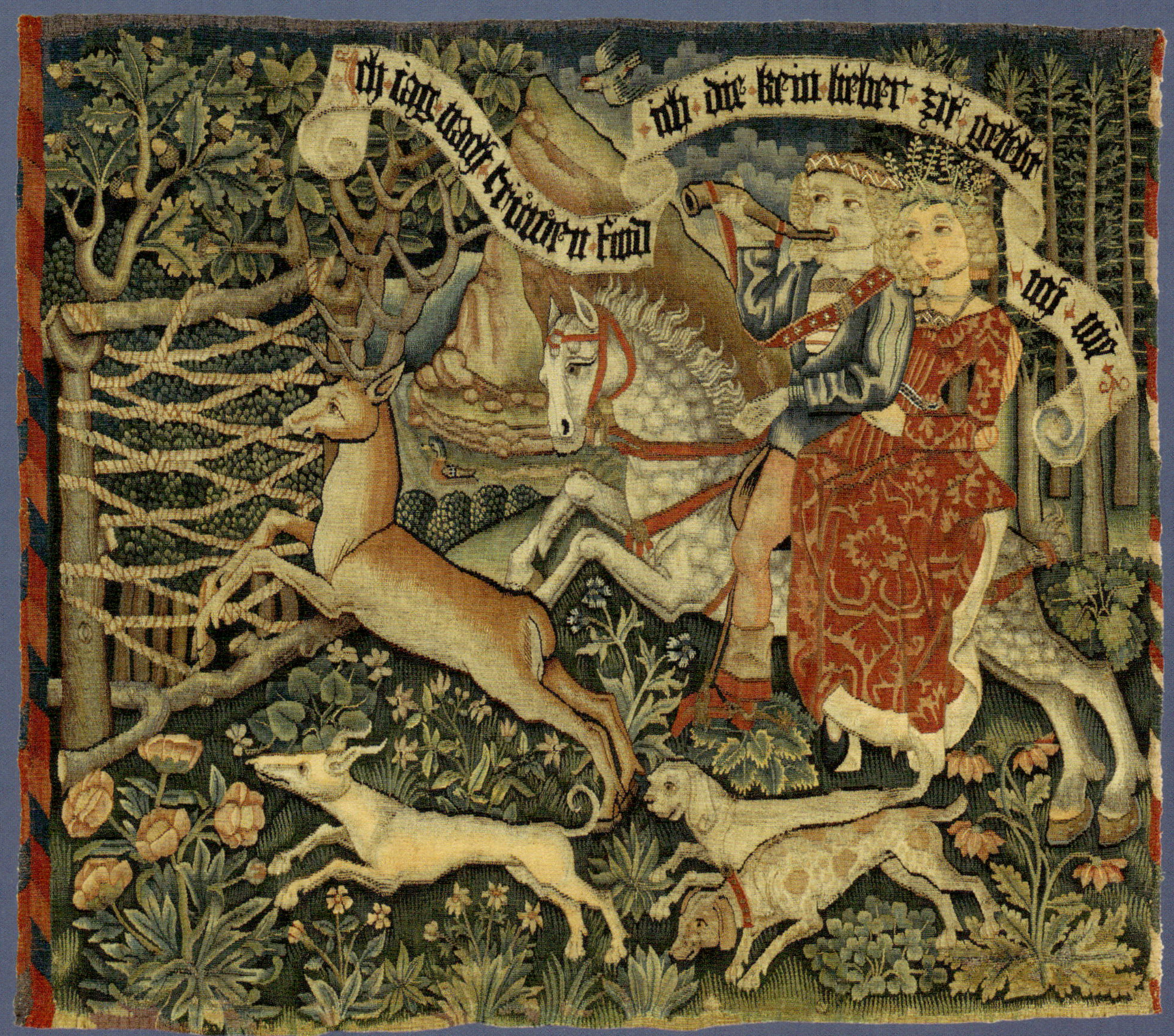

Pursuit of Fidelity, about 1480–90
Made in Alsace
Wool, linen, silk, metal thread
80 cm x 88 cm
46.28

While many hunting scenes on tapestries depict rural pursuits, some such as this one, also convey an allegorical meaning. Here the young aristocratic couple on horseback accompanied by hounds chase a hart into a net, however, the banderol or scroll above reads 'I hunt for fidelity; if this I find, I ask for nothing more'. William Burrell hung this tapestry paired with that showing David and Bathsheba, shown opposite, in the No.1 guest bedroom at Hutton Castle, Berwickshire.

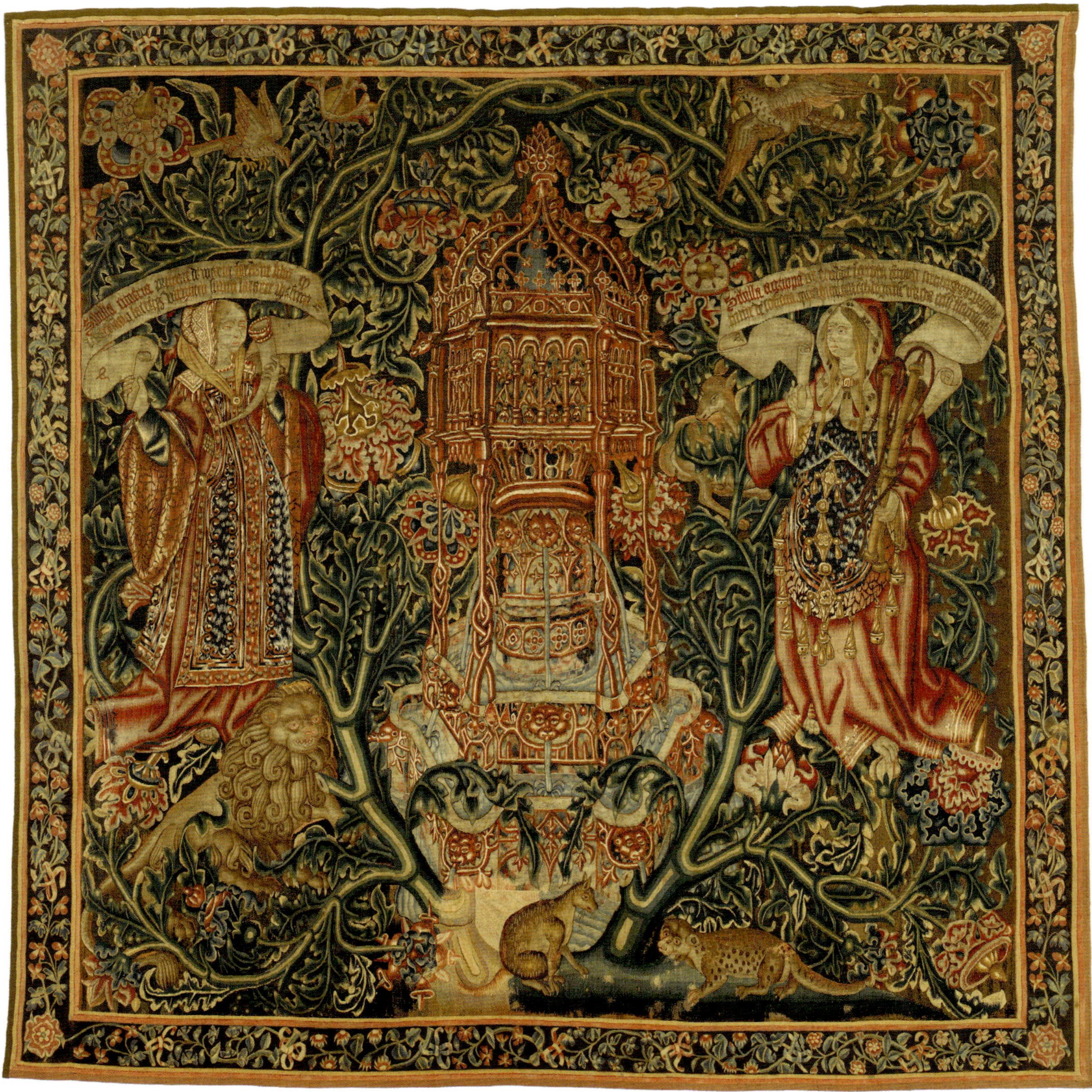

Sibylla Cimeria and Sibylla Agippa, after 1481
Probably made in Enghien, Southern Netherlands
Wool, silk
325 cm x 316 cm
46.139

Sibyls were oracles or prophetesses in Ancient Greece who were the subject of renewed interest during the Middle Ages. The Italian scholar Filippo Barbieri (1426–87) in his *Sibyllarum et prophetarum de Christo vaticinia*, 1481, paired the female sibyls to the male Old Testament prophets arguing that they too predicted episodes in Christ's life. Sibylla Cimeria's cornucopia-shaped vessel alludes to the Virgin and Child, while Sibylla Agippa's whip foretells the flagellation of Christ. Sibylla Europa, who was originally woven to stand opposite another Sibylla, holds a sword in reference to the Massacre of the Innocents.

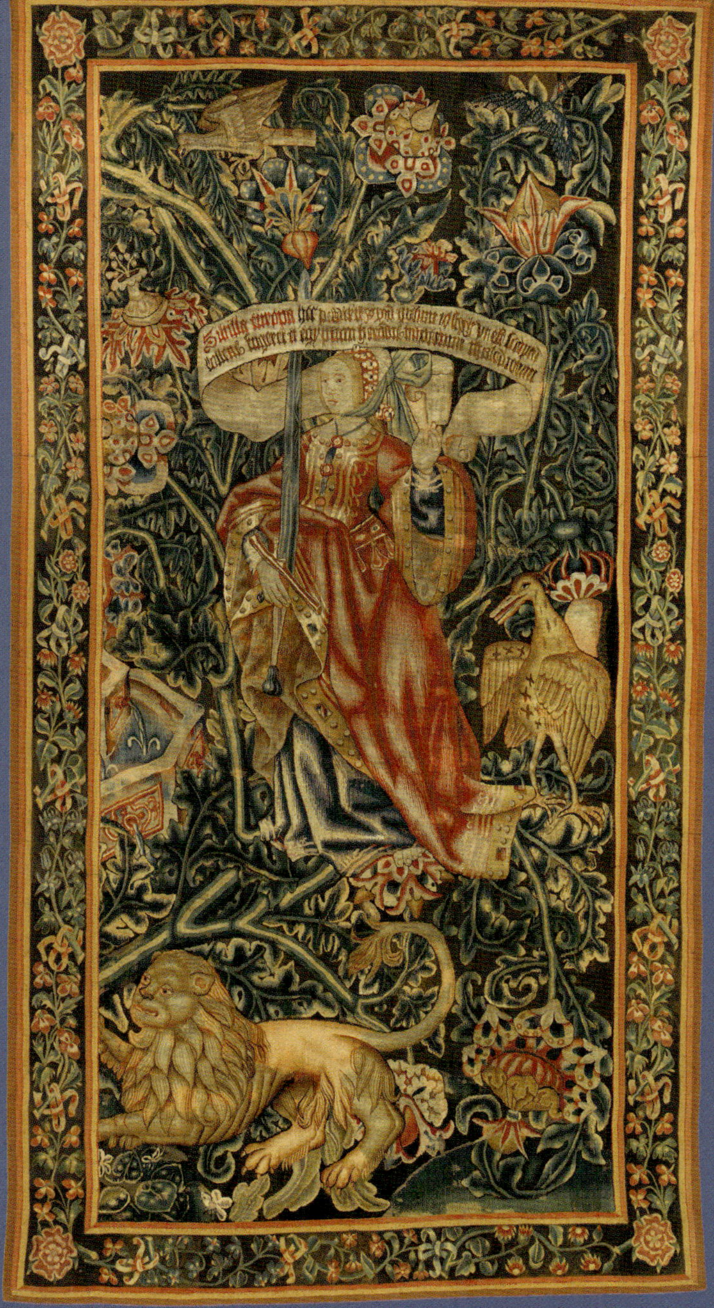

Sibylla Europa, after 1481
Probably made in Enghien, Southern Netherlands
Wool, silk
327 cm x 172 cm
46.134

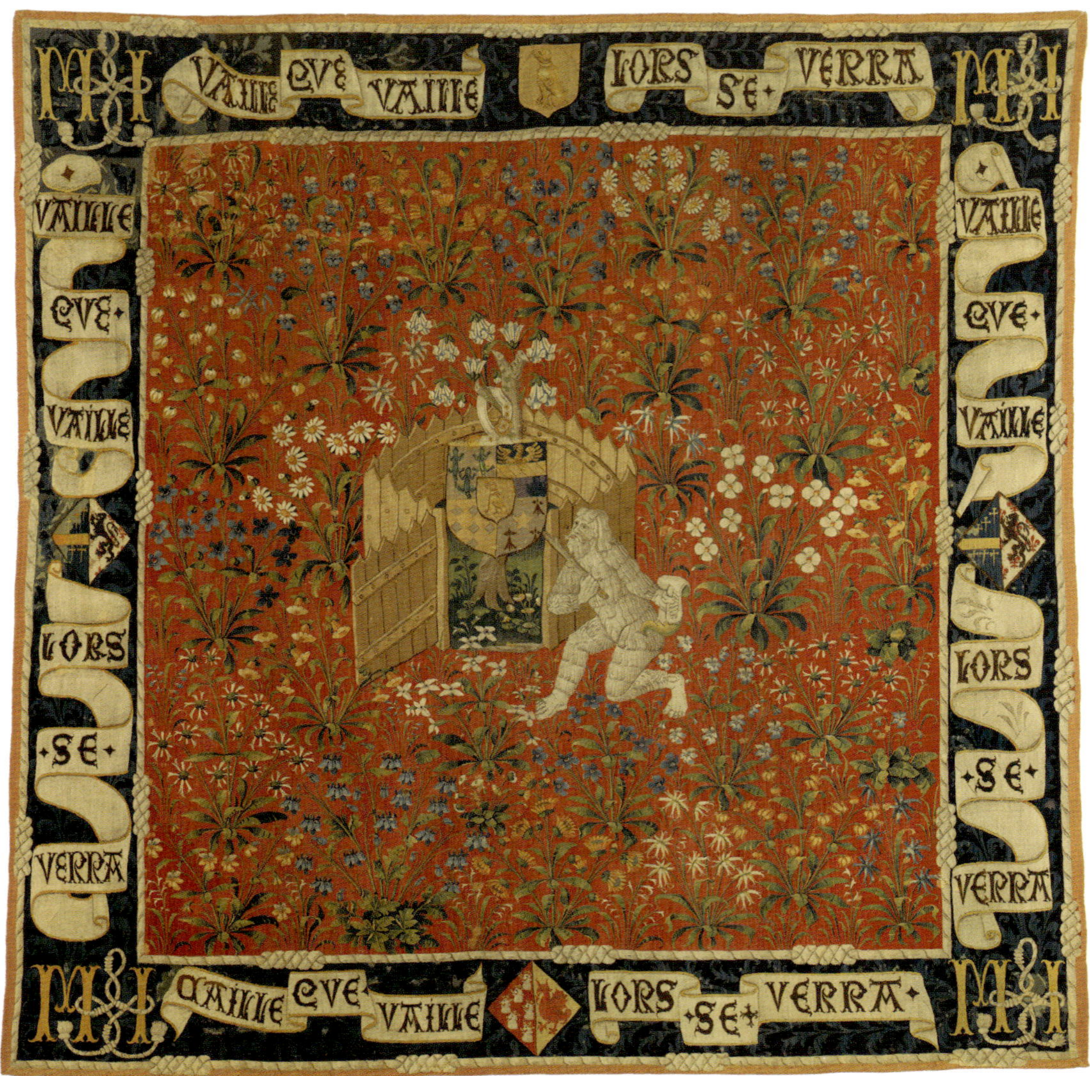

Wild Man Guarding a Coat of Arms,
about 1485
Possibly made in Paris, France or Bruges,
Brabant, Southern Netherlands, now Belgium
Wool
310 cm x 305 cm
46.103

This is one of two tapestries made for the Brachet family of Orléans, France. Due to their strength wild men often appear as guards or supporters on coats of arms. Its pendant or pair, *Griffin Guarding a Coat of Arms,* is now in the Detroit Institute of Arts, America. Both feature striking backgrounds of scattered flowers known as *mille-fleurs* or thousand flowers, a style that was popular during the late 1400s and early 1500s. Their borders include the arms of other French families and the motto '*Vaille que vaille, lors se verra*', which translates as 'Come what may, we shall see'.

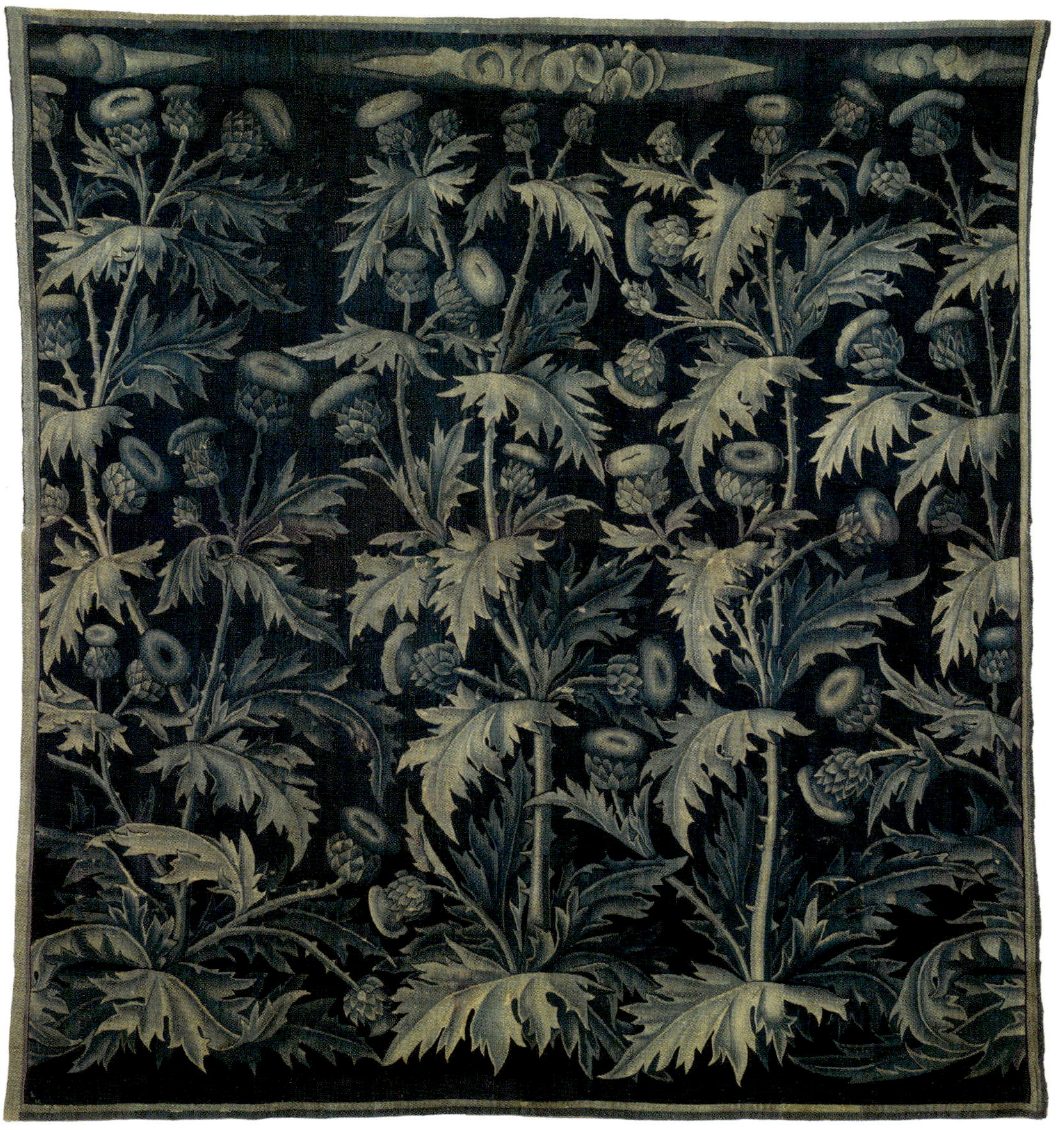

Verdure with Thistles, about 1490–1520
Made in Brussels, Brabant, or Bruges, Flanders,
Southern Netherlands, now Belgium
Wool
271 cm x 249 cm
46.108

Verdure means 'lush green vegetation' and sets
of tapestries depicting tastefully arranged foliage
were popular for creating harmonious interior
decoration schemes during the late 1400s and
early 1500s. While the thistles on this tapestry appear
naturalistic they are not botanical representations of
any known species of thistle. Another tapestry that
was probably from this set is now in the Danish Museum
of Art and Design, Copenhagen. A different set
featuring thistles is known to have been commissioned
by Margaret of Austria (1480–1530) in 1509, and
another by her nephew Charles of Habsburg (1500–88),
later Holy Roman Emperor in 1518.

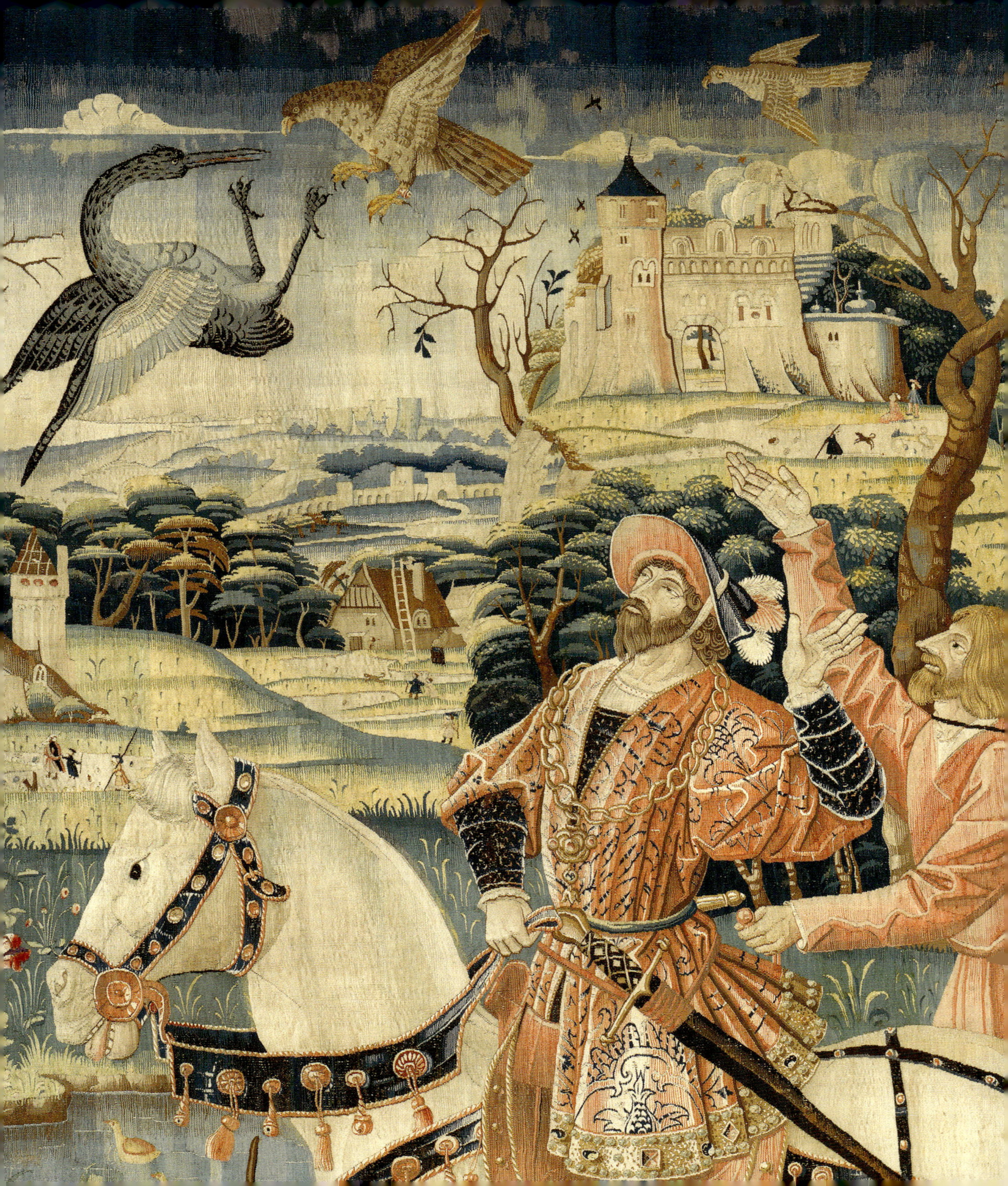

Sixteenth-century Tapestries

Tapestry workshops flourished during the early sixteenth century as European monarchs acquired grand sets to decorate their Renaissance palaces. To ensure that no king was outdone by another, series were often made in multiples so that each ruler could add one to their growing collections. The most impressive were those of the Holy Roman Emperor Charles V (1500–88), Francis I of France (1494–1547) and Henry VIII of England (1491–1547). The inventories of the latter alone record that he owned over 2,000 tapestries, including ones previously belonging to the disgraced Cardinal Thomas Wolsey (about 1474–1530).

This consumption of tapestries trickled down to noble families, who as well as purchasing items from stock would often commission designs that promoted their family's wealth and connections, such as the notable Luttrell Carpet (pp.60–61). Medieval styles, such as *mille-fleurs* or thousand flower tapestries, continued to be woven, but Renaissance art was also influencing designs with artists, such as Bernard van Orley (1487/91–1541), using perspective and naturalistic backgrounds in their tapestry cartoons.

In part influenced by the historic houses of sixteenth-century gentry and contemporary country house style, the Burrells lived with their tapestries on display. At 8 Great Western Terrace, Glasgow, Burrell's early purchases were hung or mounted on the walls, including *Charity Overcoming Envy* on the first floor staircase. In 1916 Burrell bought Hutton Castle, near Berwick-upon-Tweed. As well as showcasing tapestries in the principal reception rooms, such as the hall and drawing room, the Burrells also decorated the private guest and family rooms with them. Frank Surgey (1893–1980) was employed by Burrell to fit out the interiors at Hutton Castle. Through the firm Acton Surgey Ltd, of which he was a partner, Surgey also sold several tapestries to Burrell, including the portrait of Vincenz von Schleinitz, Bishop of Merseburg, in 1933.

Opposite: The use of perspective with its muted colours and reducing size of the buildings not only makes this appear naturalistic, but also helps the viewer to focus on the action in this dynamic scene. *Fight between a Falcon and a Heron* (detail; see also p. 54).

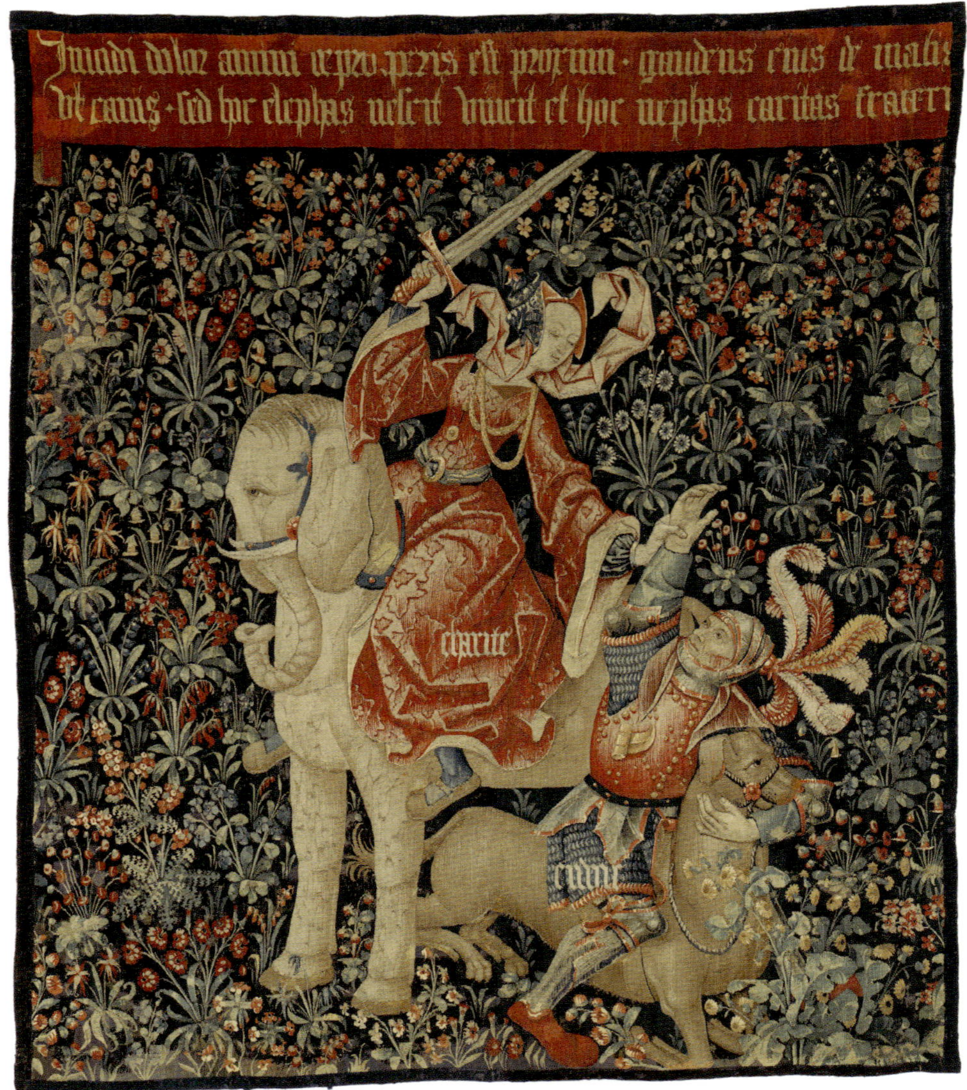

Charity Overcoming Envy, about 1500
Probably made in Brussels, Brabant,
Southern Netherlands, now Belgium
Wool, silk
254 cm x 216 cm
46.95

This allegorical tapestry shows an unusual
depiction of Charity, which is one of the three
Theological Virtues along with Faith and Hope.
Normally Charity is shown triumphing over
Greed and Kindness conquering Envy, however,
here Charity overcomes Envy. It is also noticeable
for depicting Charity riding an elephant rather
than a horse.

This tapestry was lent by Sir Thomas David
Gibson-Carmichael (1859–1926) to the Glasgow
International Exhibition in 1901; he sold it at
auction the following year. Burrell acquired it then
or soon after and displayed it on the landing at
8 Great Western Terrace. Later it was displayed
in the Drawing Room at Hutton Castle,
Berwickshire.

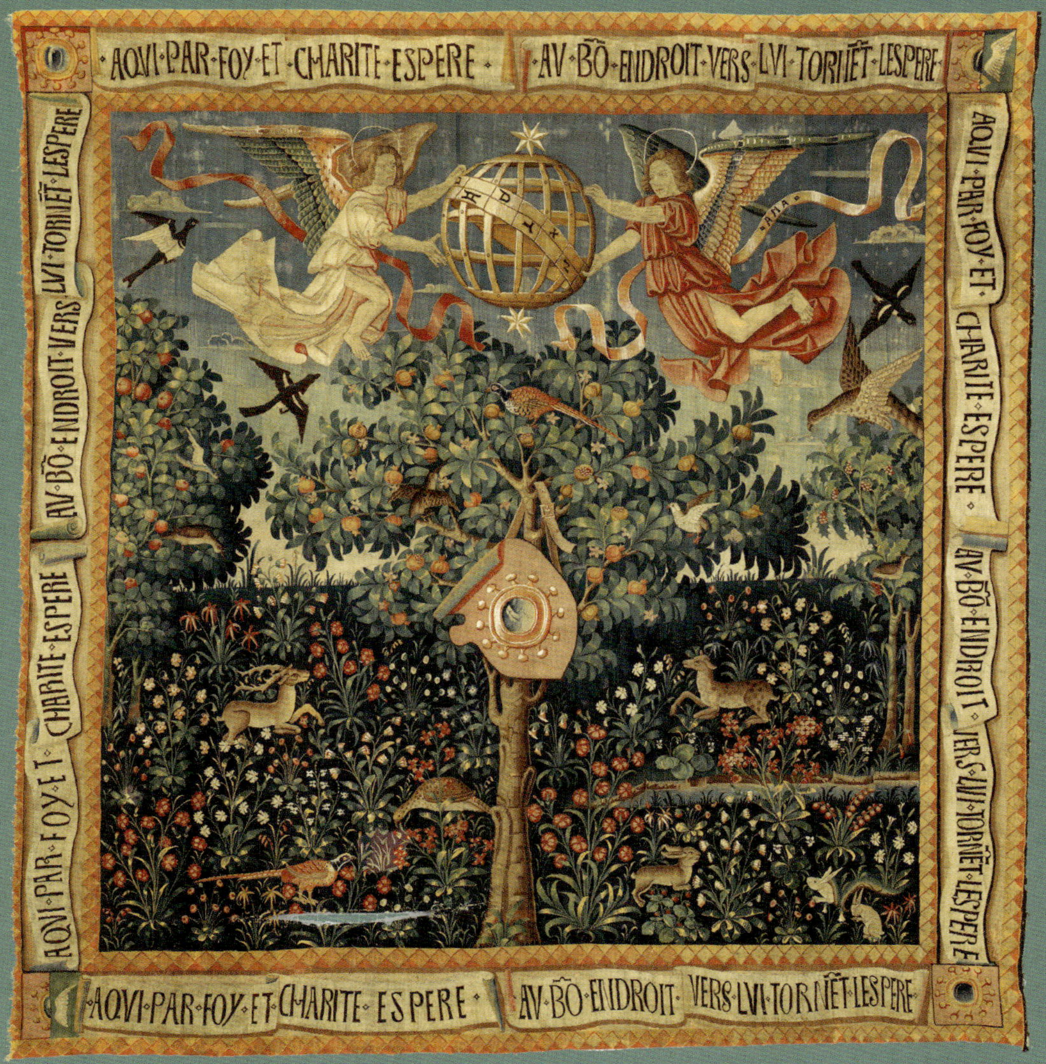

Landscape with the Arms of the Miro Family, about 1500

Probably made in Paris, France or Bruges,
Flanders, Southern Netherlands, now Belgium
Wool, silk
354 cm x 336 cm
46.102

At the top of this beautiful tapestry two angels
hold an armillary sphere with the motto 'To he
who places his hopes in faith and charity, the
spheres will turn favourably'. Astronomy was
associated with medicine during the 1600s and
whilst the positioning of the zodiac is incorrect, the
arrangement may have held a meaning to the original
owners. The tapestry was probably commissioned for
Gabriel II Miro, doctor and councillor to Kings Louis
XII (1462–1515) and Francis I of France or his father
Francois Miro, who served Charles VIII (1470–98).
The mirror in the centre of their coat of arms is a
visual pun on their surname, Miro.

Object in Focus

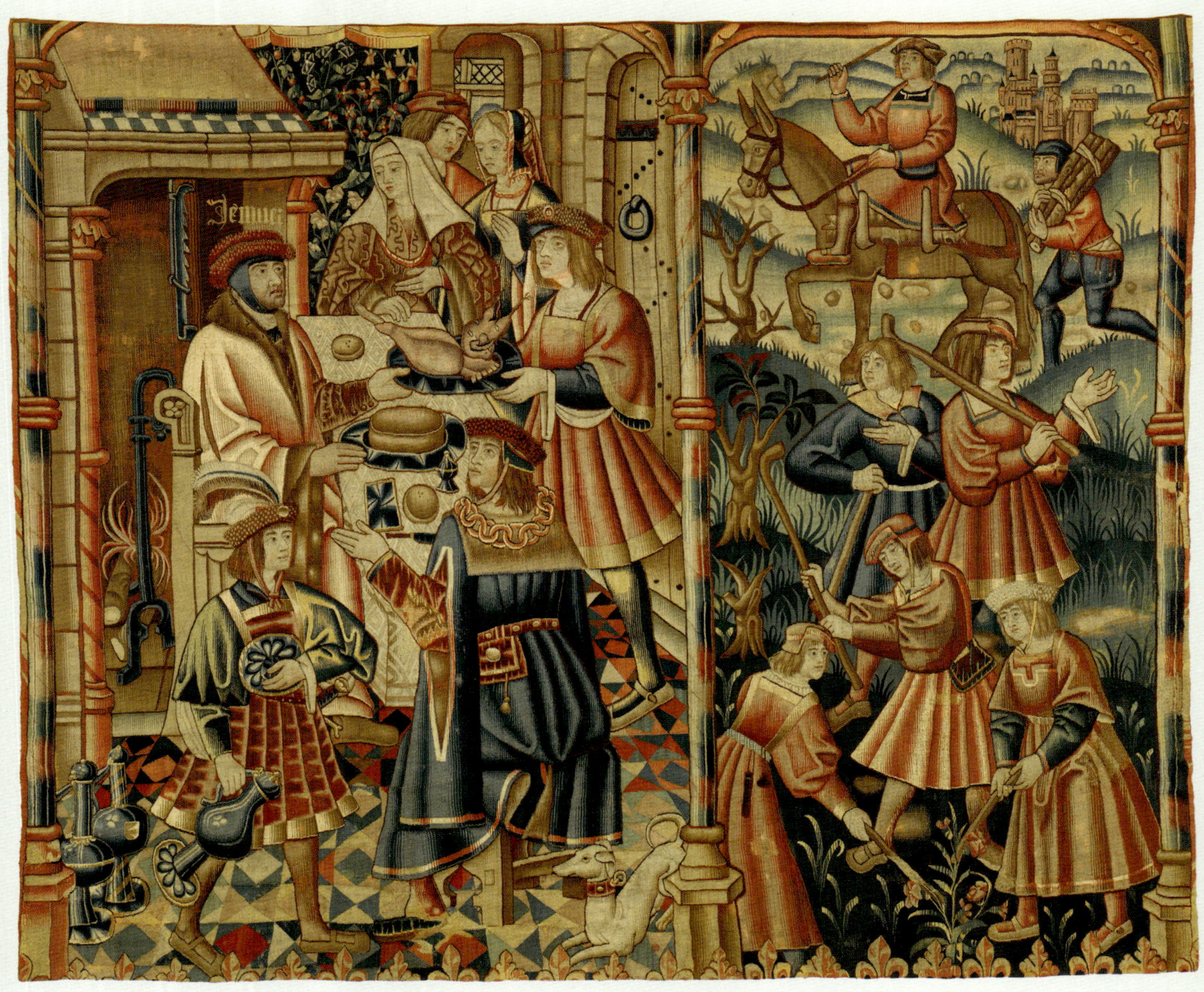

The Months: January, about 1500
Possibly made in Tournai, Hainault,
Southern Netherlands, now Belgium
Wool, silk
276 cm x 328 cm
46.75

Illustrated scenes showing activities relating to each month of the year were often found in devotional Books of Hours, such those by the Limbourg brothers in the *Très Riches Heures*, about 1412–16, made for John, Duke of Berry. By the late Middle Ages these scenes were also found in interior decorating schemes, from small stained and painted glass roundels mounted in windows to large tapestries hanging on the walls.

In many of these images January is depicted showing a man sitting indoors in front of a fire. On this tapestry that scene is expanded to show the man, a visitor, being offered hospitality by a wealthy family on the left as a good omen for the year ahead, whilst outside five men play hockey.

This is one of three tapestries from this series, along with ones representing April and September, which were lent by Mrs Isabella Burrell (1834–1923) to the Glasgow International Exhibition in 1901. The following year her son William and his wife, Constance, hung the trio in the dining room of their new marital home at 8 Great Western Terrace. The three were later displayed at Hutton Castle, suggesting they were amongst Burrell's favourite tapestries.

The Months: January on display in the Drawing Room at Hutton Castle, Berwickshire. Glasgow Museums Archive, GMA.2013.1.1.1095

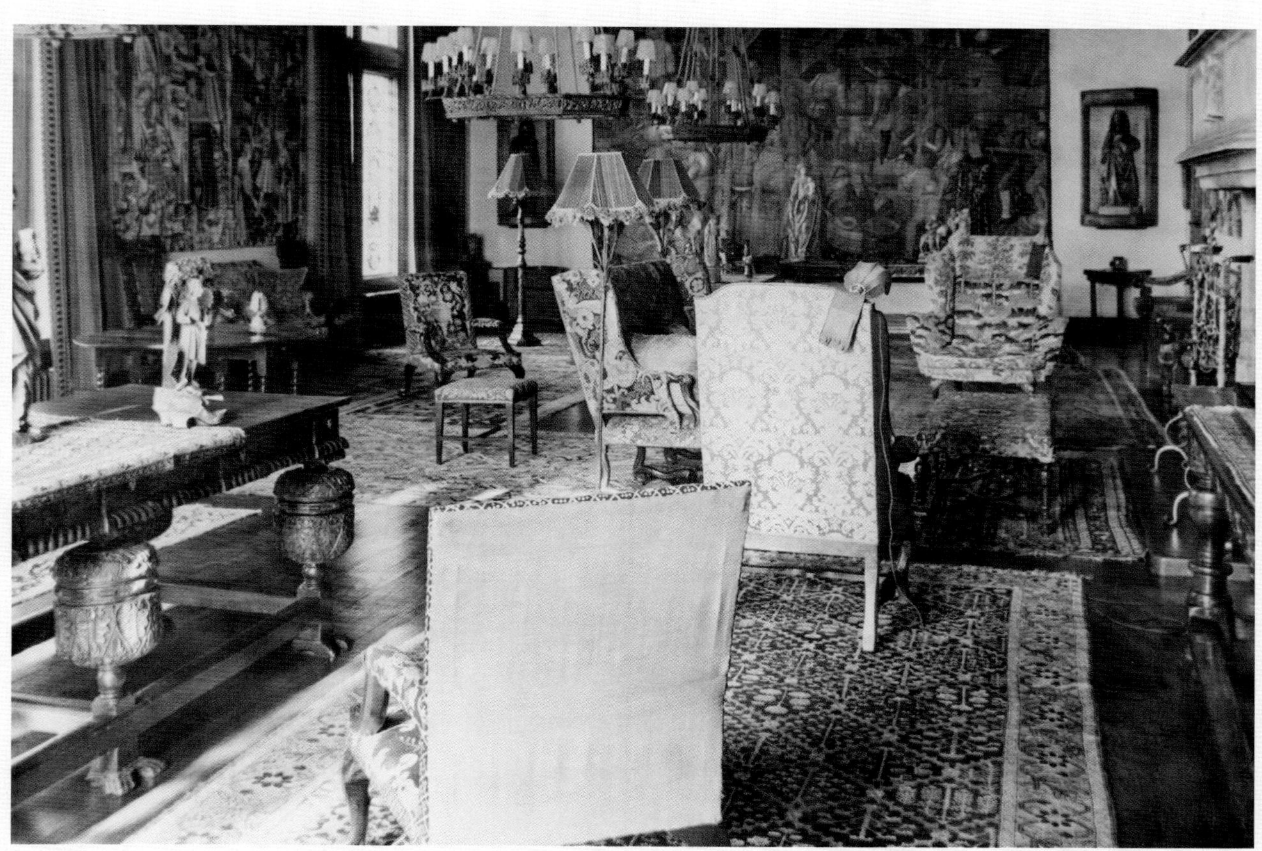

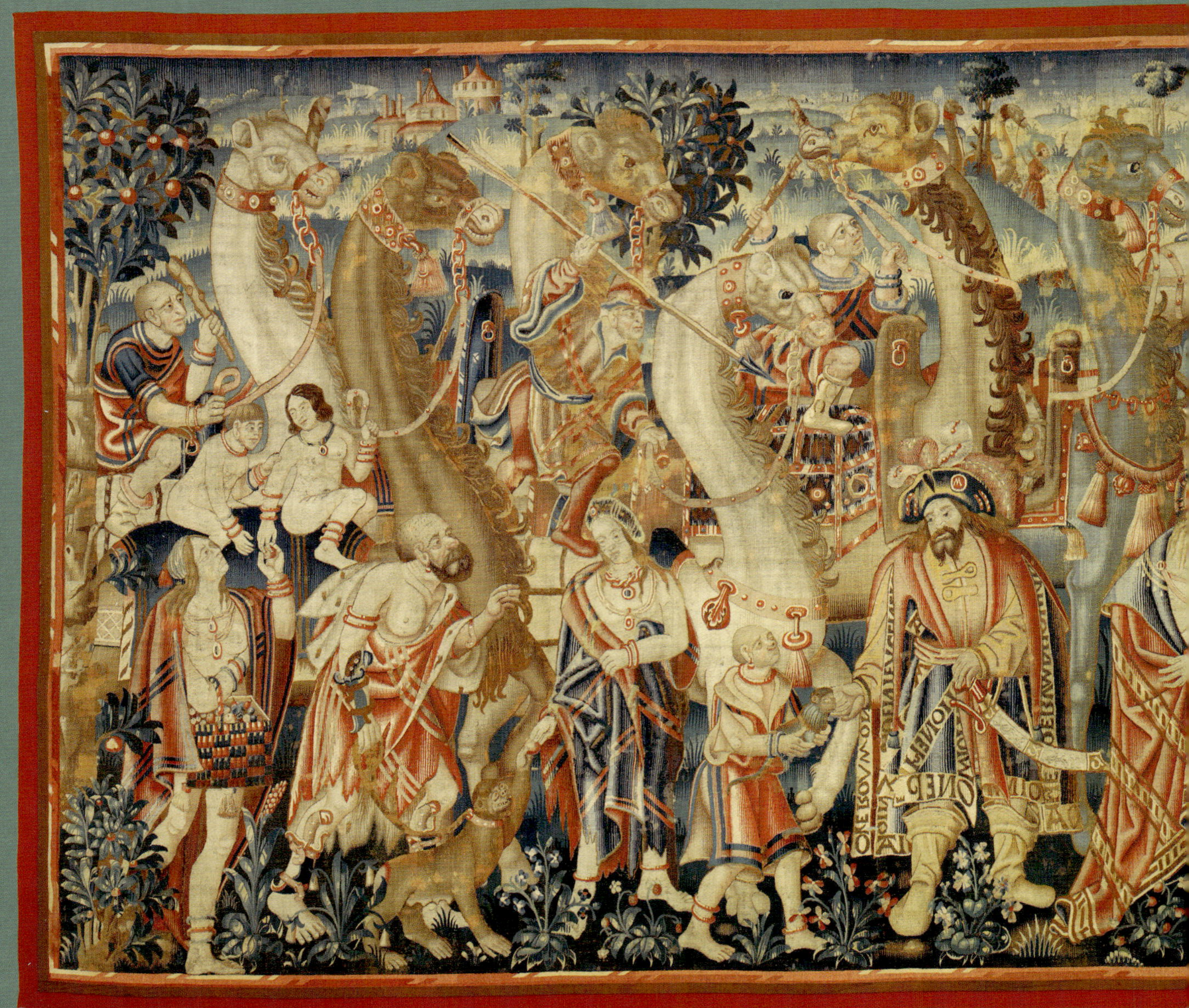

Exploration of the Indies: The Camel Caravan,
about 1500–30
Made in the workshop of Arnould Poissonier, possibly Tournai,
Hainault, Southern Netherlands, now Belgium
Wool, silk
360 cm x 652 cm
46.94

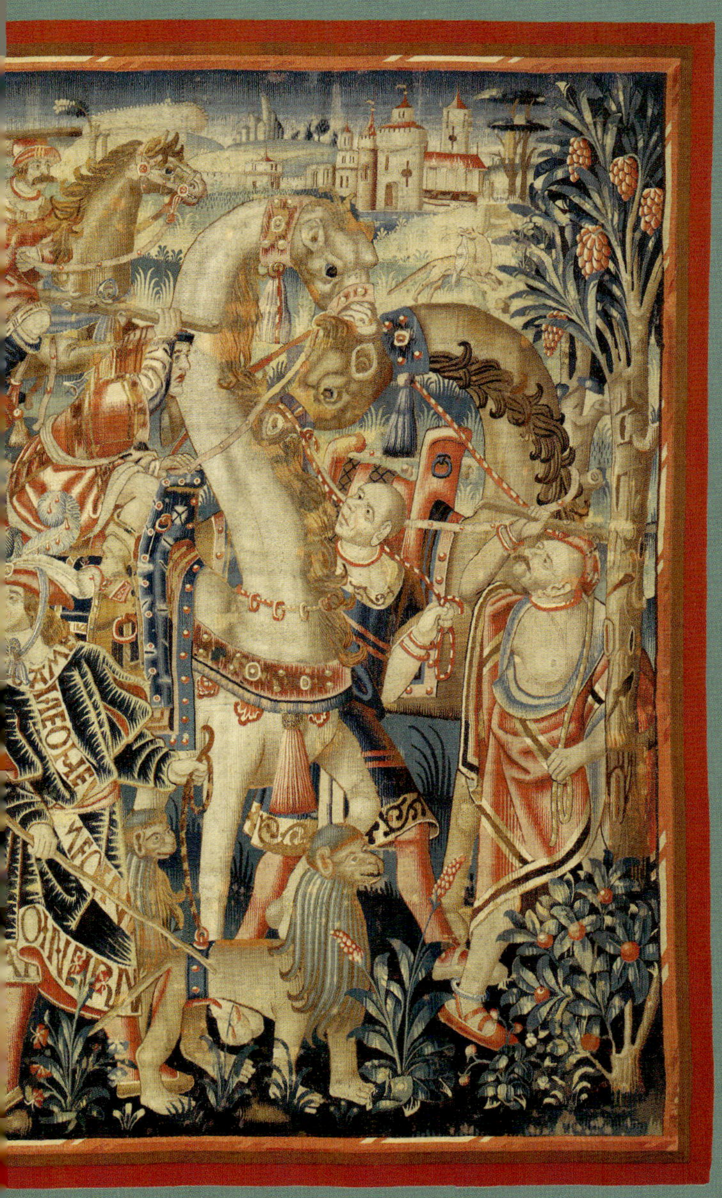

This large tapestry is from a series of possibly 10 tapestries known as the *Voyage de Caluce* (Voyage to Calicut) made to celebrate the voyages of Portuguese explorer Vasco da Gama (d. 1524), who led the first European expeditions to India in 1497–99 and 1502–03. As well as showing Da Gama's embarkation from Lisbon, arrival in Calicut and return, the series also shows stops en route and some of the exotic animals given to or collected by the Portuguese. Here it is camels, their extended necks filling the height of the tapestry. In another scene it is naturally long-necked giraffes that are depicted.

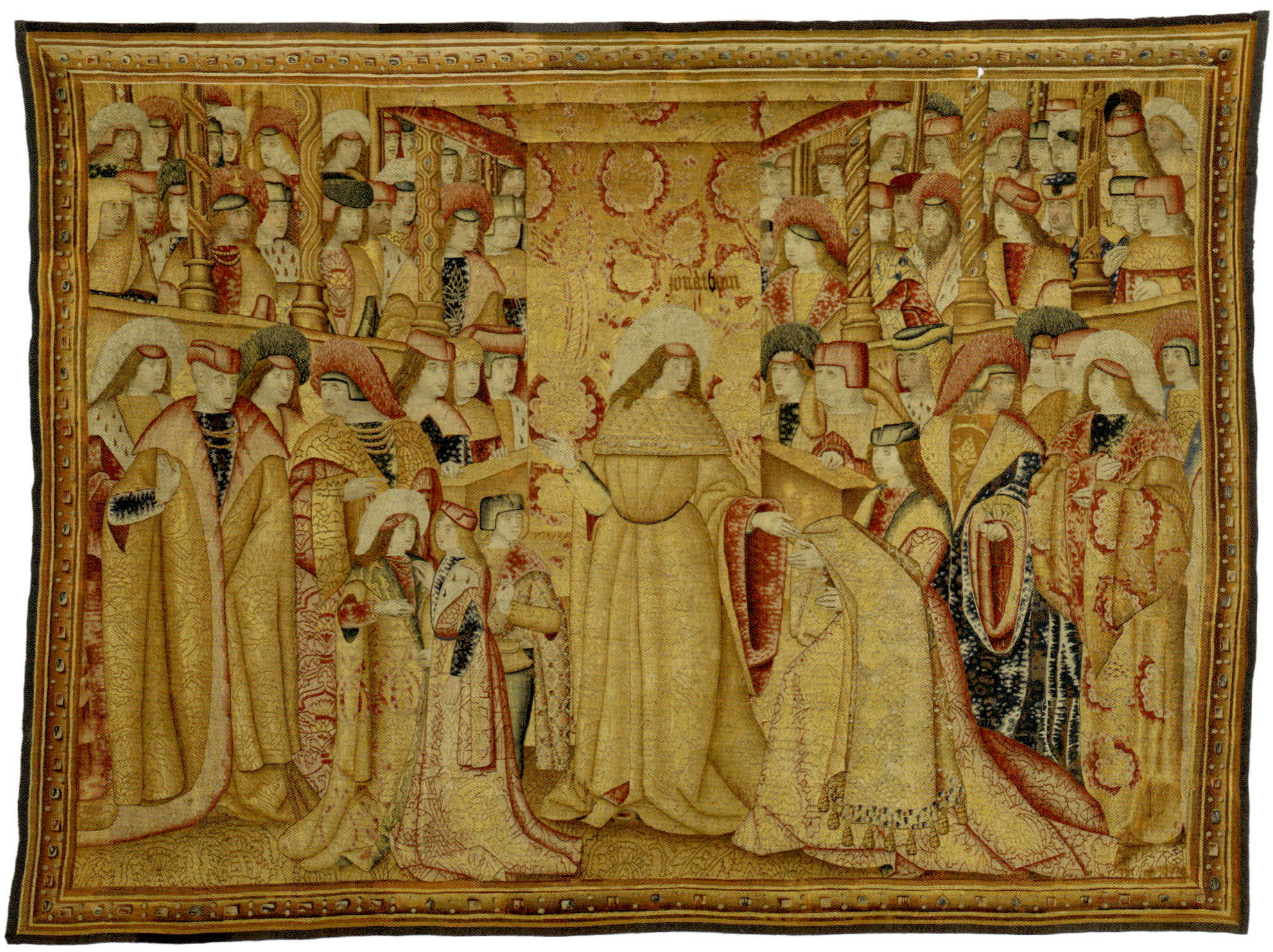

**Jonathan Maccabeus receiving the robe
from Alexander Balas,** about 1515
Made in Southern Netherlands, now Belgium
Wool, silk
315 cm x 410 cm
46.116

The story of Jonathan Maccabeus (d. 143 BC)
appears in the Old Testament. Maccabeus was an
unusual subject for tapestries, with no references to
this subject appearing in surviving inventories. In this
first scene from the series Jonathan receives a luxurious
robe from Alexander Balas (d. 145 BC), ruler of the
Greek Seleucid Kingdom, and is named High Priest
of Judea. Some of the proportions of the figures are a
little odd, such as Jonathan's head which is too small
in relation to his body, suggesting that the designer
was reusing cartoons from other tapestries to create
the scenes in this series.

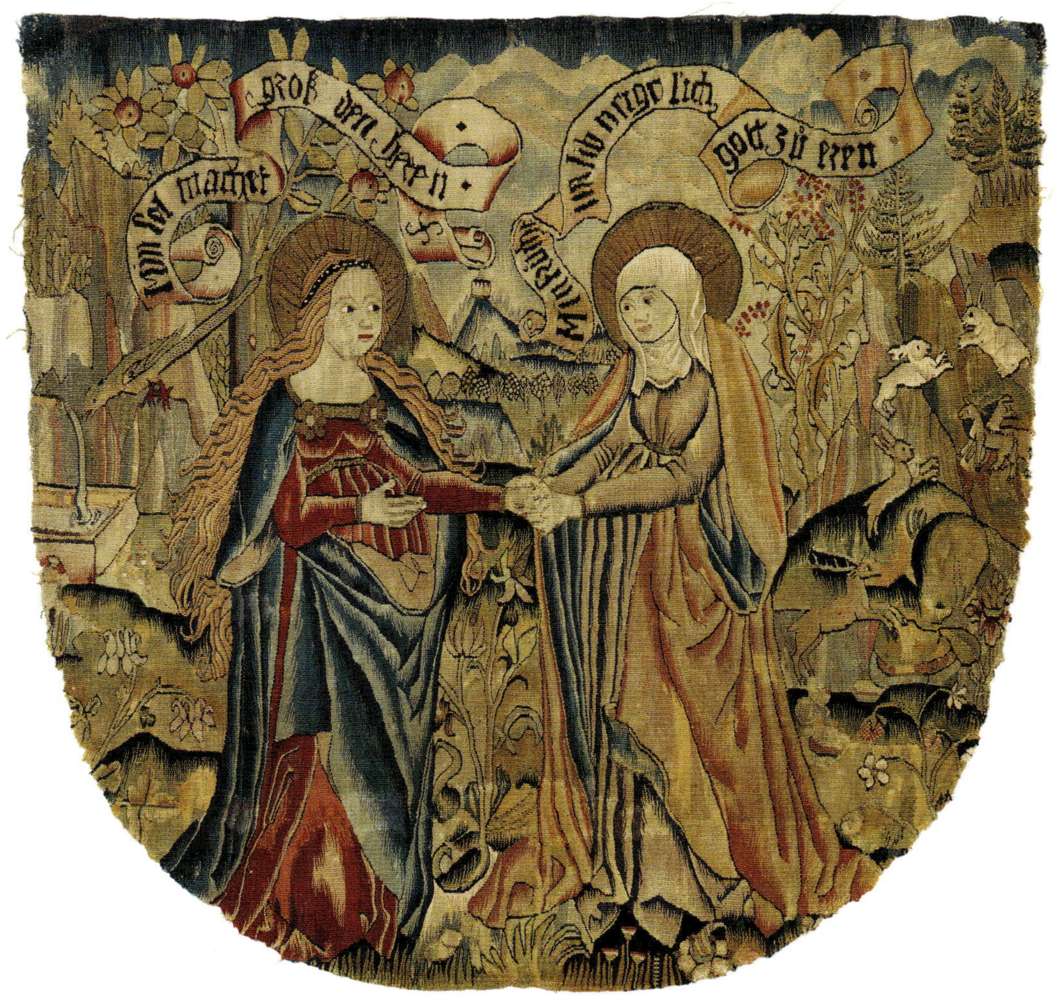

The Visitation, about 1510–20
Made in Alsace
Linen, silk, wool, metal thread
78 cm x 81 cm
46.45

Here the Virgin Mary, pregnant with Jesus
Christ, seeks the advice of her older cousin
Elizabeth, who is pregnant with her son John,
who became St John the Baptist. William
Burrell purchased this tapestry from John Hunt,
a London-based dealer, in 1938. Burrell's
Purchase Book entry briefly describes the
piece, but makes no reference to its history.
Burrell may not have known, but we now know
that this was part of the forced sale of the Jewish
collector Emma Budge's collection in Berlin,
Germany, in 1937. Following government advice
and international protocols regarding Nazi war
loot, Glasgow City Council made a payment to
her heirs in 2015 by way of compensation.

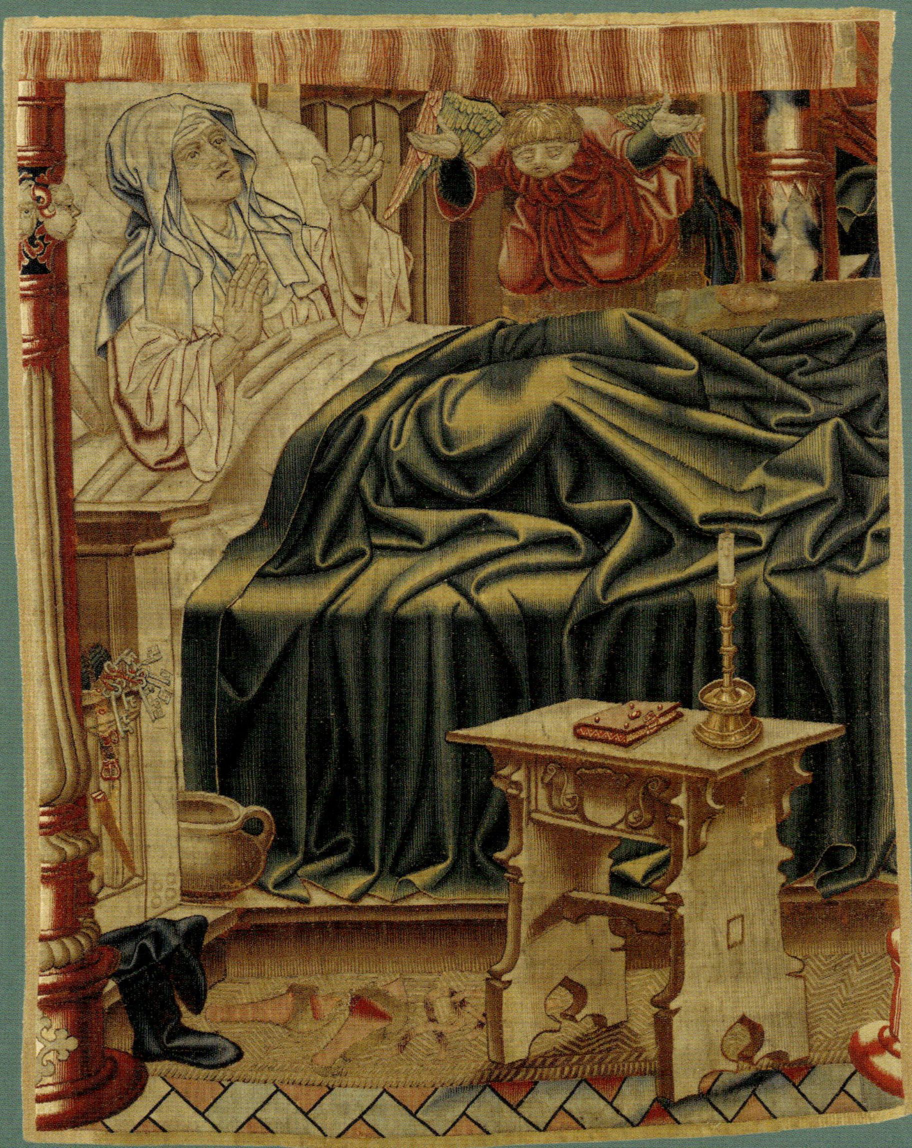

This fragment once formed the bottom left corner of a larger tapestry from a four-piece set depicting the Legend of Our Lady of the Sands. The series narrates the history of Beatrix Soetkens, a pious spinster living in Antwerp, who received miraculous visions of the Virgin Mary in 1348. The first vision appeared when Beatrix was in bed and was depicted above the fringed bed valance before the tapestry was cut up in the late 1800s.

When William Burrell bought this piece in 1938 the subject was incorrectly identified as St Anne. As a result, Burrell paid the relatively low price of £385 for the tapestry.

The Legend of Our Lady of the Sands:
Beatrix Soetkens in Bed, about 1516–18
Designed by Bernard van Orley, probably made in
Brussels, Brabant, Southern Netherlands,
now Belgium
Wool, silk
163 cm x 127 cm
46.126

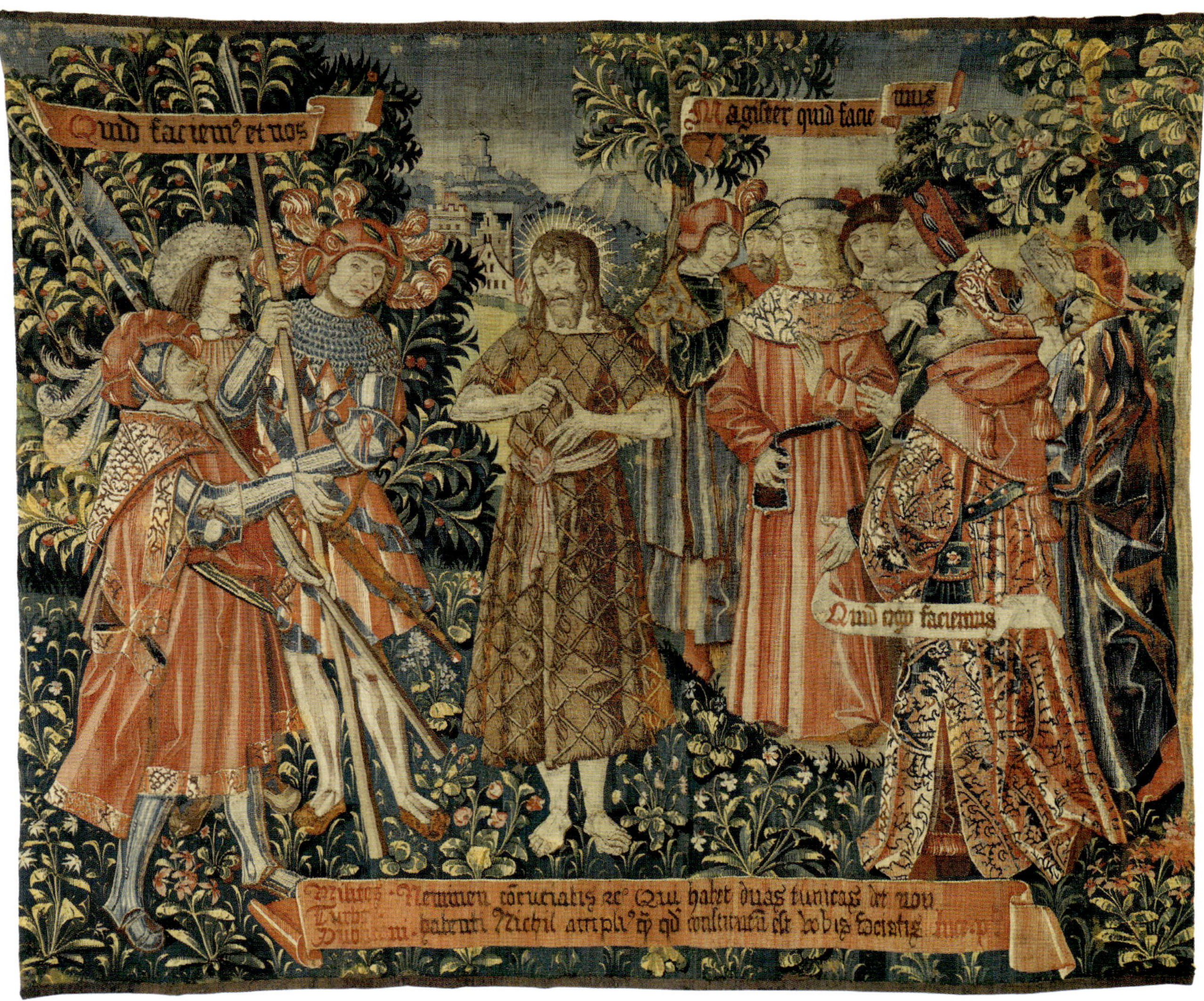

Scenes from the Life of John the Baptist: The Baptist Preaching to the People, the Publicans and the Soldiers, 1516–21

Made in the workshop of Guillaume de Rasse, Paris, France
Wool, silk
175 cm x 208 cm
46.124

Originally made to decorate a choir stall, this is a section of a series of tapestries showing the life of John the Baptist. Here John is asked, 'What shall we do?' and replies in turn 'He that has two coats, let him give to him that has none', 'Do nothing more than that which is appointed you' and 'Do violence to no man'.

When William Burrell bought objects he noted in his Purchase Books if they had been published previously. Here, the entry states that this tapestry had been illustrated in G.J. Demotte, *La Tapisserie Gothique* (Gothic Tapestry), 1924.

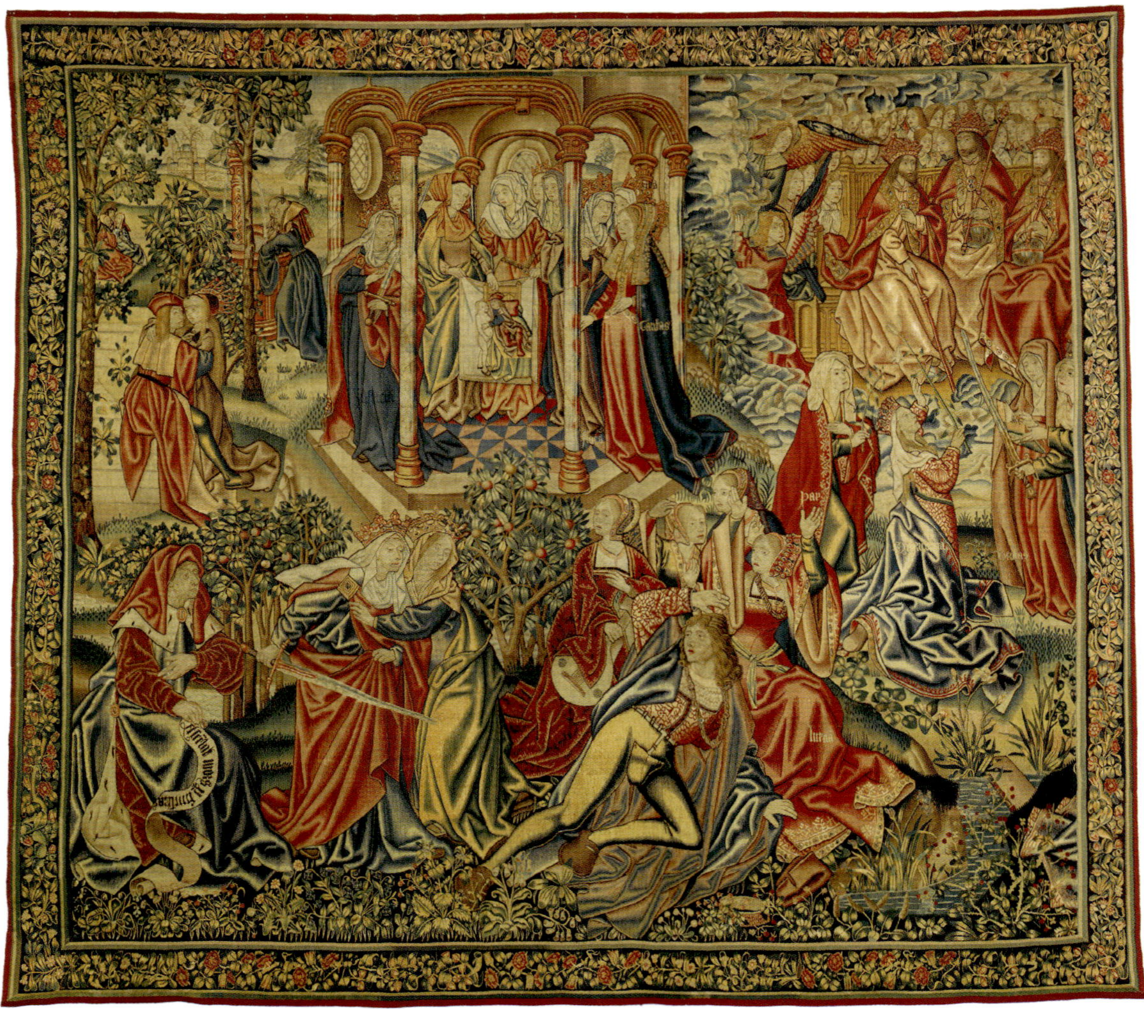

Peace and Mercy Petition for the Redemption of Mankind, about 1520

Possibly made in Brussels, Brabant, Southern Netherlands, now Belgium
Wool, silk
422 cm x 467 cm
46.127

This is the third scene from a series of 10 tapestries showing the allegorical Story of the Redemption of Man that when complete extended to over 90 metres long. At least 15 editions of the series were woven, including sets for Henry VII of England and Cardinal Thomas Wolsey.

In the top left corner a man cavorts while a tearful lady presents a depiction of lustful betrayal to the Virtues. Opposite in the top right Peace, Mercy, Truth and Justice kneel before the Holy Trinity. In the foreground, the Prophet Jeremiah watches Mercy attempt to restrain Justice, who is punishing a dissolute man lying on Lechery's lap.

Vincenz von Schleinitz was Bishop of
Merseburg in Saxony-Anhalt from 1526
until his death in 1535. During his lifetime
he acquired great personal wealth,
some of which he used to support the
arts.

Whilst it was not unusual to include the
portraits of the donors paying for the
commission in a tapestry, people were
not often the main subject unless they
were important rulers, popes or saints.
However, this is one of two versions
featuring a full-length portrait of Bishop
Vincenz von Schleinitz. The other is in
Naumberg Cathedral, where he was
canon from 1497.

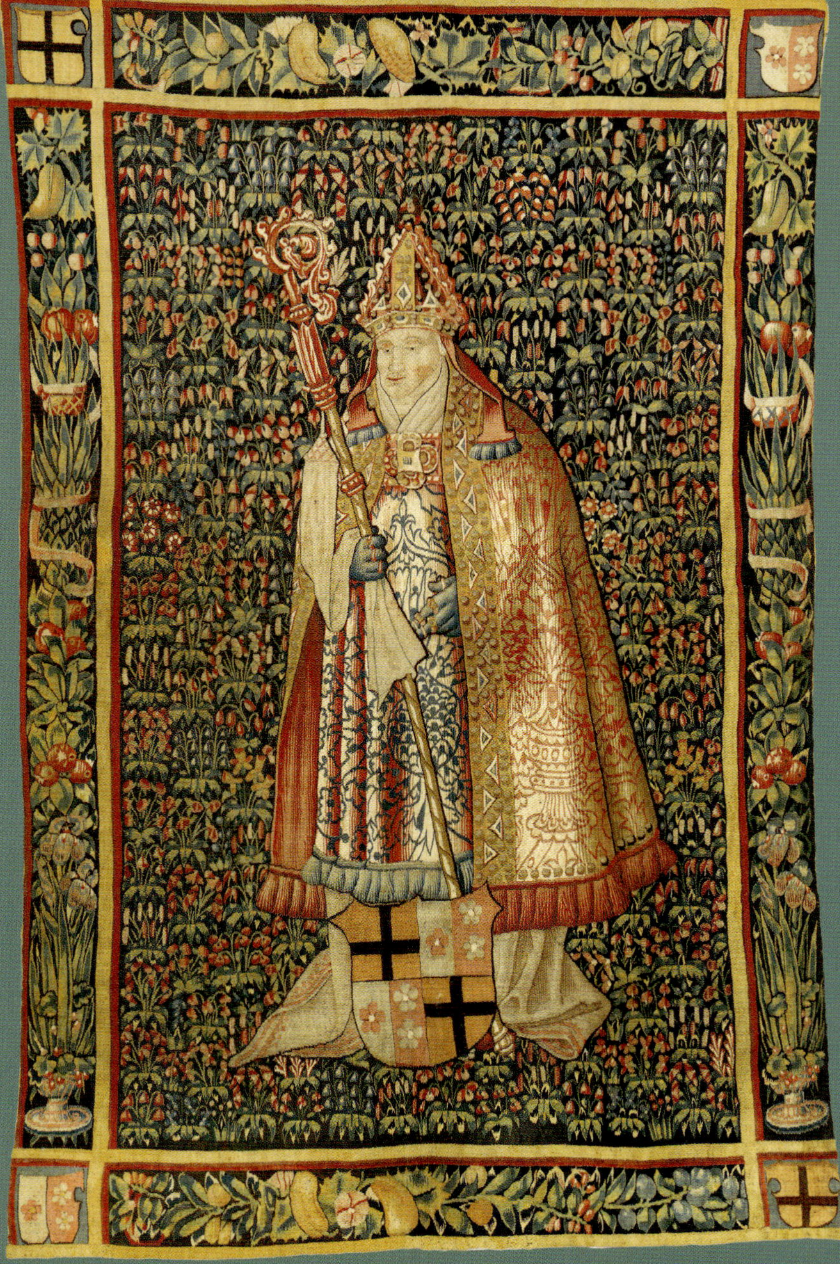

Vincenz von Schleinitz, Bishop of Merseburg, before 1535
Possibly made in Bruges, Flanders,
Southern Netherlands, now Belgium
Wool, silk
195 cm x 125 cm
46.100

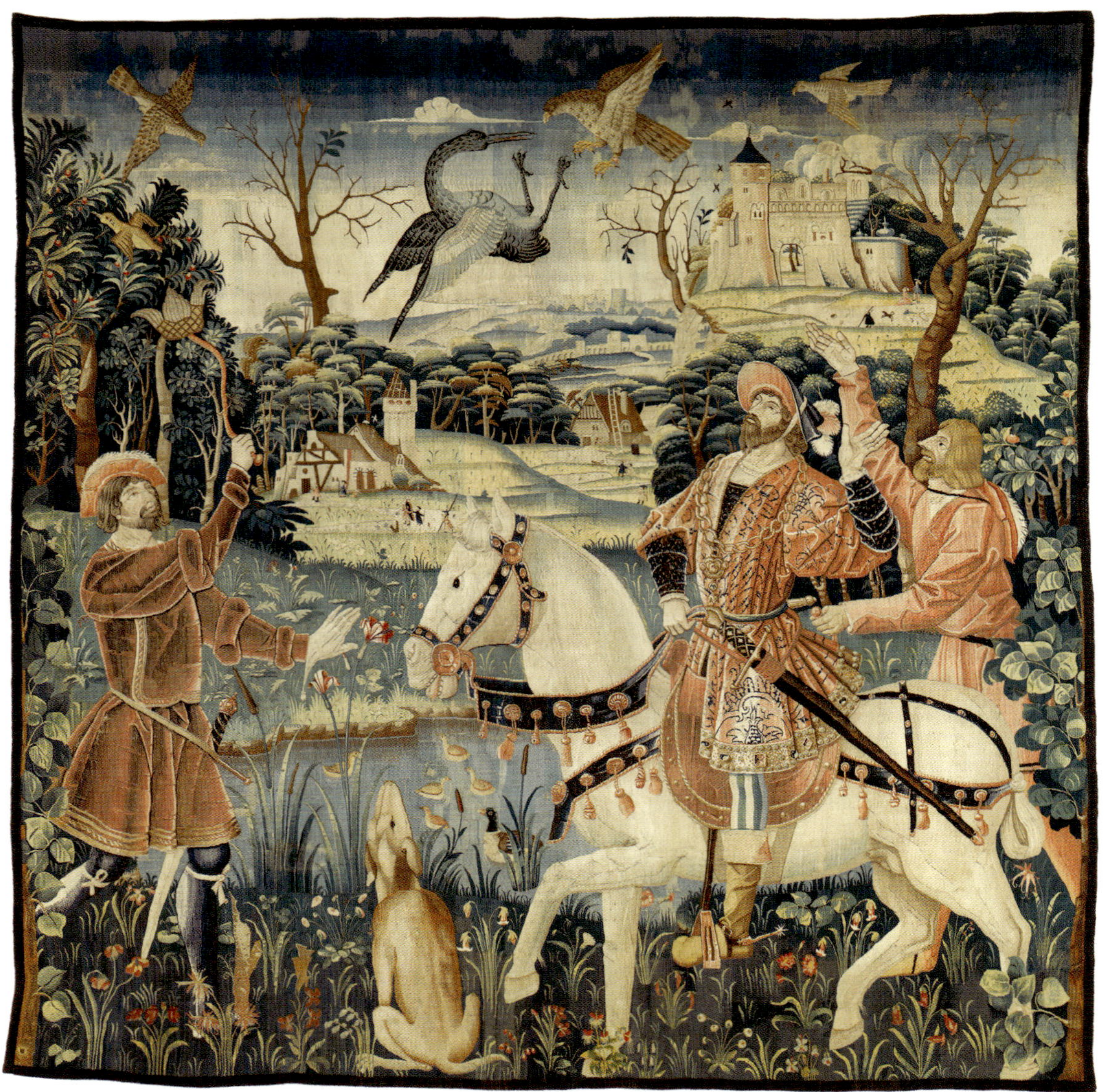

Fight Between a Falcon and a Heron,
about 1525
Probably made in Paris, France
Wool, silk
322 cm x 314 cm
46.60

Hunting scenes were a very popular subject for tapestries, especially those made speculatively for sale at trade fairs rather than as bespoke commissions. This lovely example shows a dynamic scene of an aristocratic gentleman with his falconer, another attendant and dog, enjoying what was viewed as the noble sport of falconry. On the left one falconer whirls a lure to attract the attention of a falcon, which is fighting a heron above. Due to their size and strength herons were seen to be formidable prey for falcons, providing the onlookers with an exciting spectacle to watch.

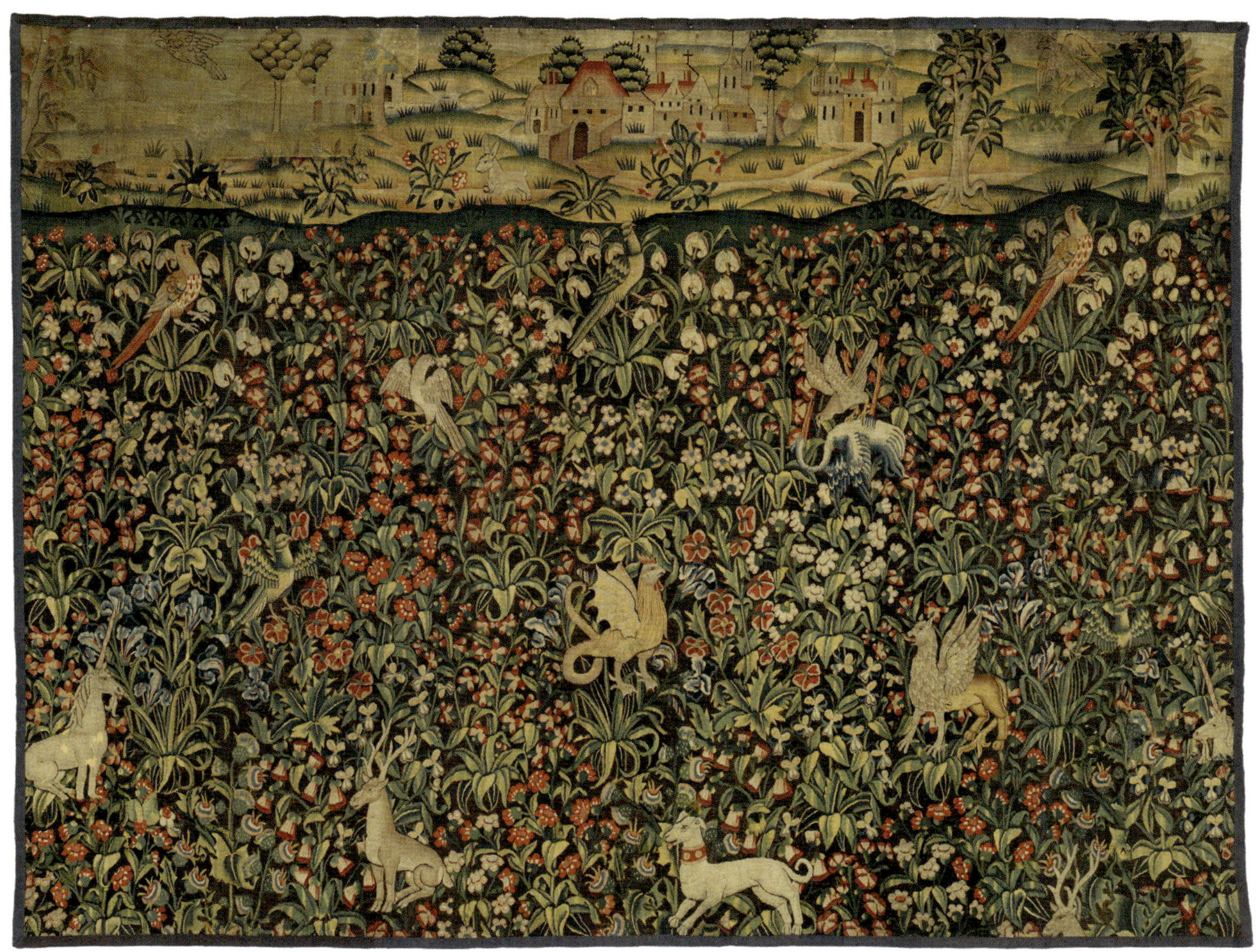

Birds and Beasts in a Landscape with a Mille-Fleurs Ground: Wyvern and Griffin,

about 1525
Possibly made in Enghien, Hainaut,
Southern Netherlands, now Belgium
Wool, silk
277 cm x 359 cm
46.105

This decorative tapestry focuses on the popular *mille-fleurs* or thousand flower ground, reducing the landscape scene above to almost a border. The dense carpet of colourful flowering plants, including blue irises and thistles, is combined with a range of real and mythological animals. One of two similar tapestries bought by William Burrell, this one features a wyvern, a two-legged dragon depicted here with a cockerel-like head, and a griffin, alongside birds, stags, unicorns and a dog.

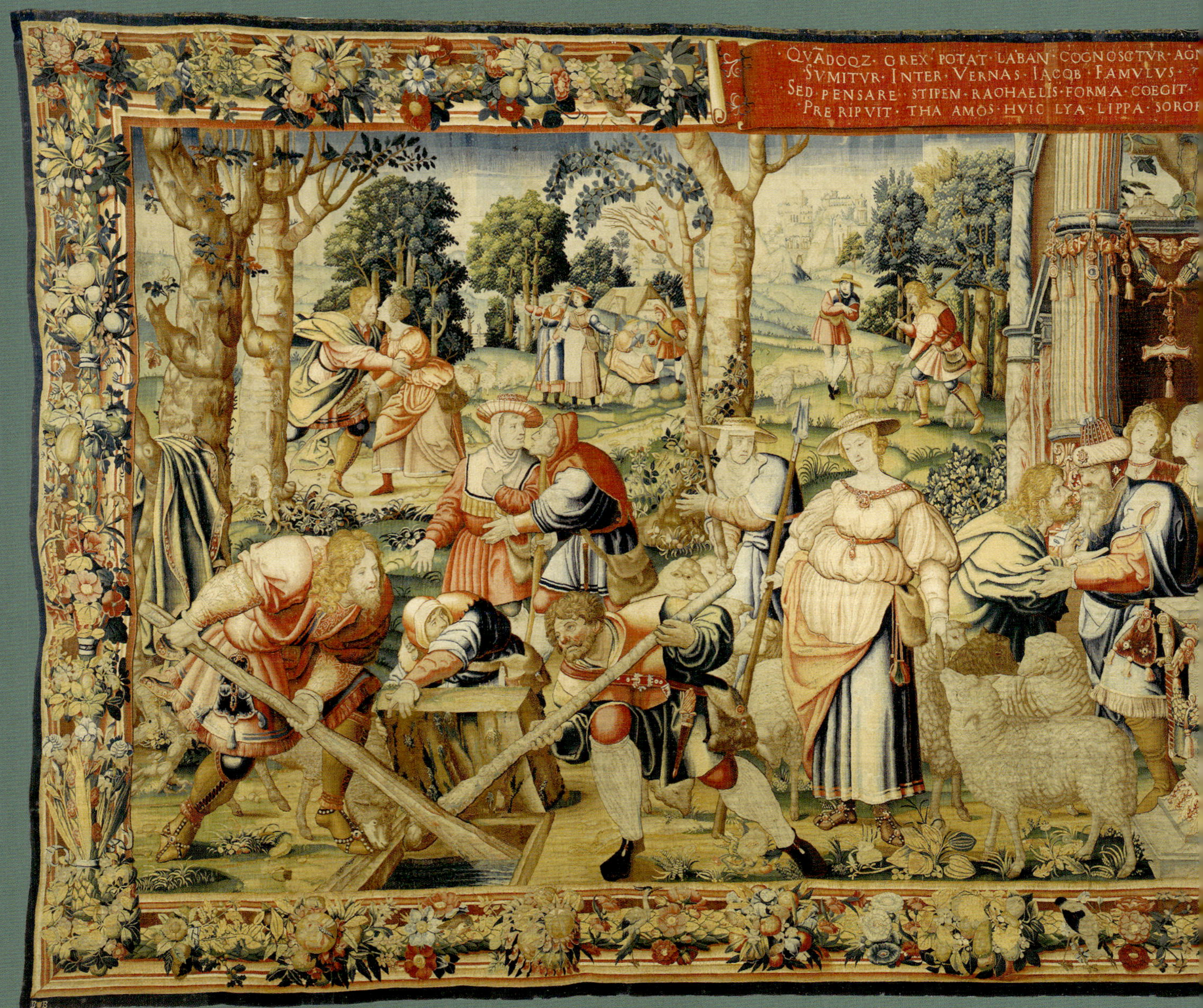

The Story of Jacob:
The Meeting and Marriage of Jacob and Rachel, about 1535–40
Designed by Bernard van Orley, made in the workshop of Willem de Kempeneer,
Brussels, Brabant, Southern Netherlands, now Belgium
Wool, silk
421 cm x 796 cm
46.110

56

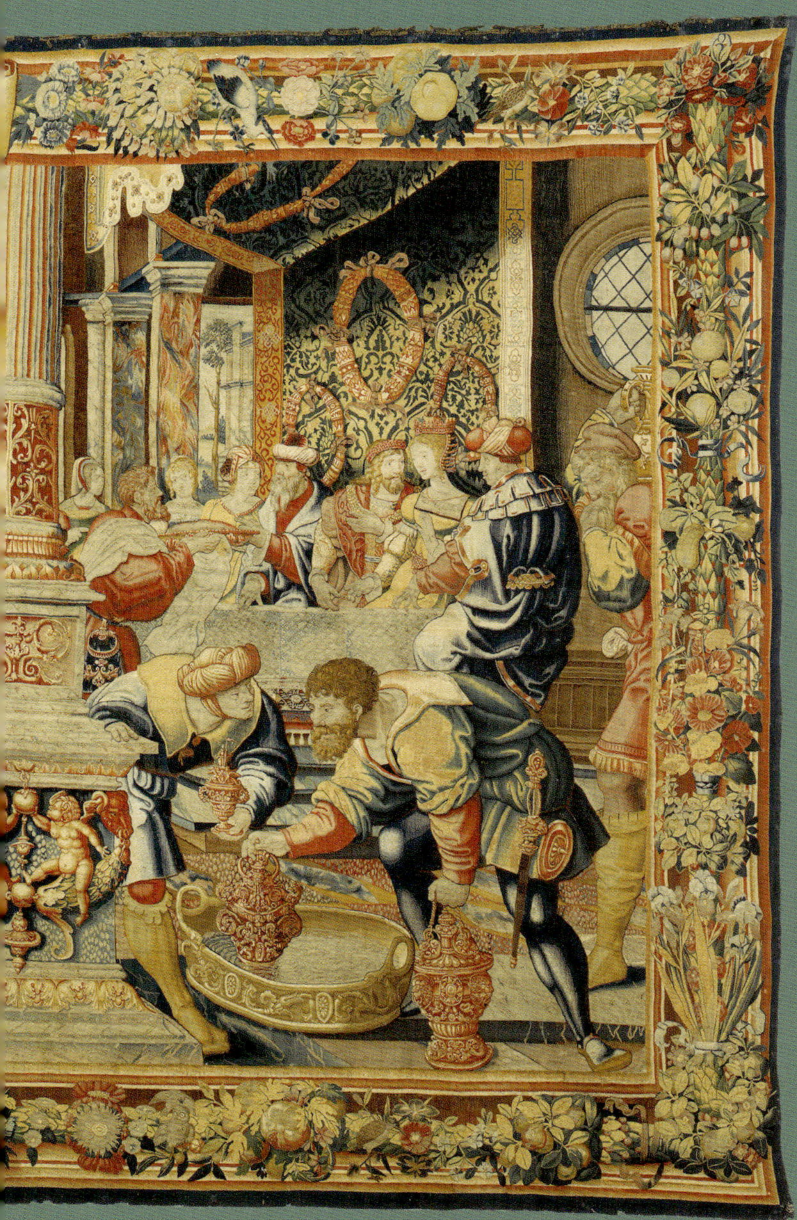

Bernard van Orley (1487/91–1541) was a Flemish artist and tapestry designer. His work was influenced by Italian Renaissance artists, as seen on this tapestry where the story of Jacob and Rachel enfolds in a series of scenes scaled to fit the perspective. In the foreground the story begins with Jacob helping to move a stone off the mouth of a well so that Rachel can give her sheep water. Receding trees on the left and columns on the right help to take the viewer's eye up to the later scene with smaller figures in the background showing Jacob tending Rachel's father Laban's flock of sheep.

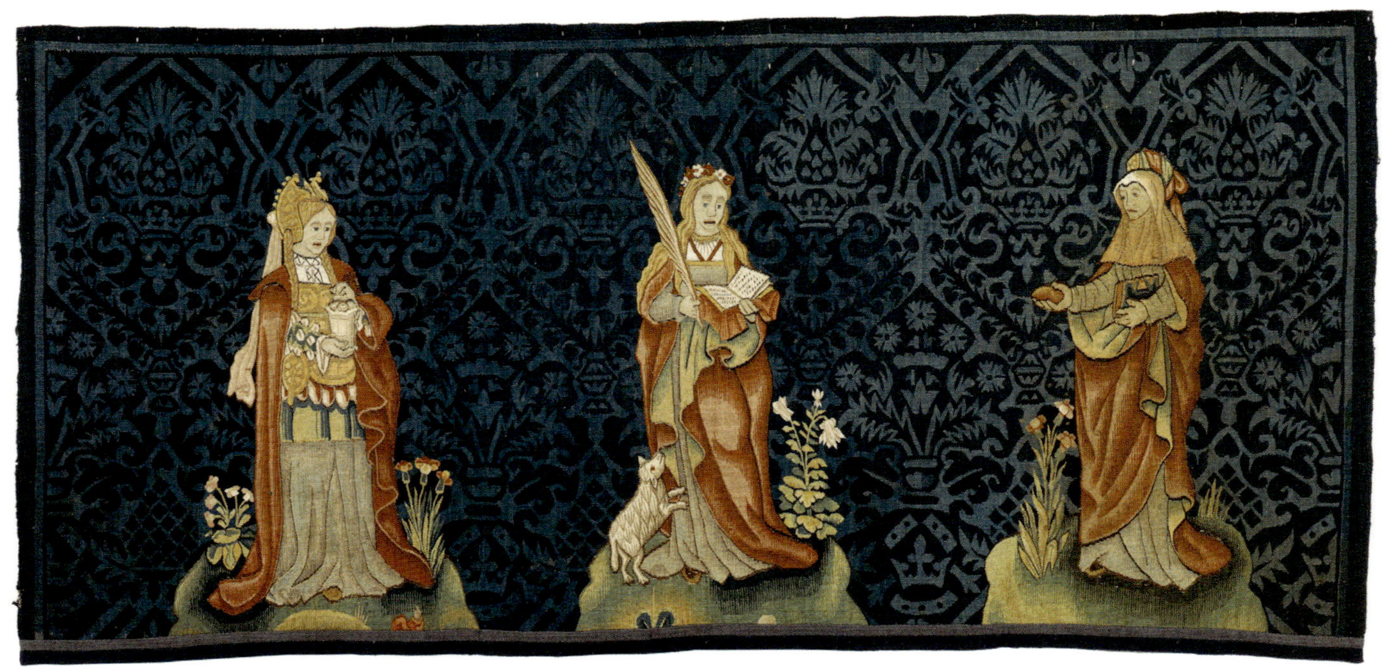

Altar Frontal with Saints Mary Magdalene, Agnes and Elizabeth of Hungary,
about 1525–50
Probably made in Sint-Truiden, Limburg,
Southern Netherlands, now Belgium
Wool, linen, silk
98 cm x 197 cm
46.125

Each of the three female saints on this altar frontal is identifiable by her attributes, the items she carries, or the animals she is shown with. On the left St Mary Magdalene holds a jar of ointment, in the centre St Agnes is accompanied by a lamb and on the right St Elizabeth is carrying a loaf of bread. This was in the Church of St Agnes Beguinage, Sint-Truiden, Belgium until at least 1905, along with a similar tapestry showing St Catherine, the Virgin of the Apocalypse and St Barbara now in the Metropolitan Museum of Art, New York.

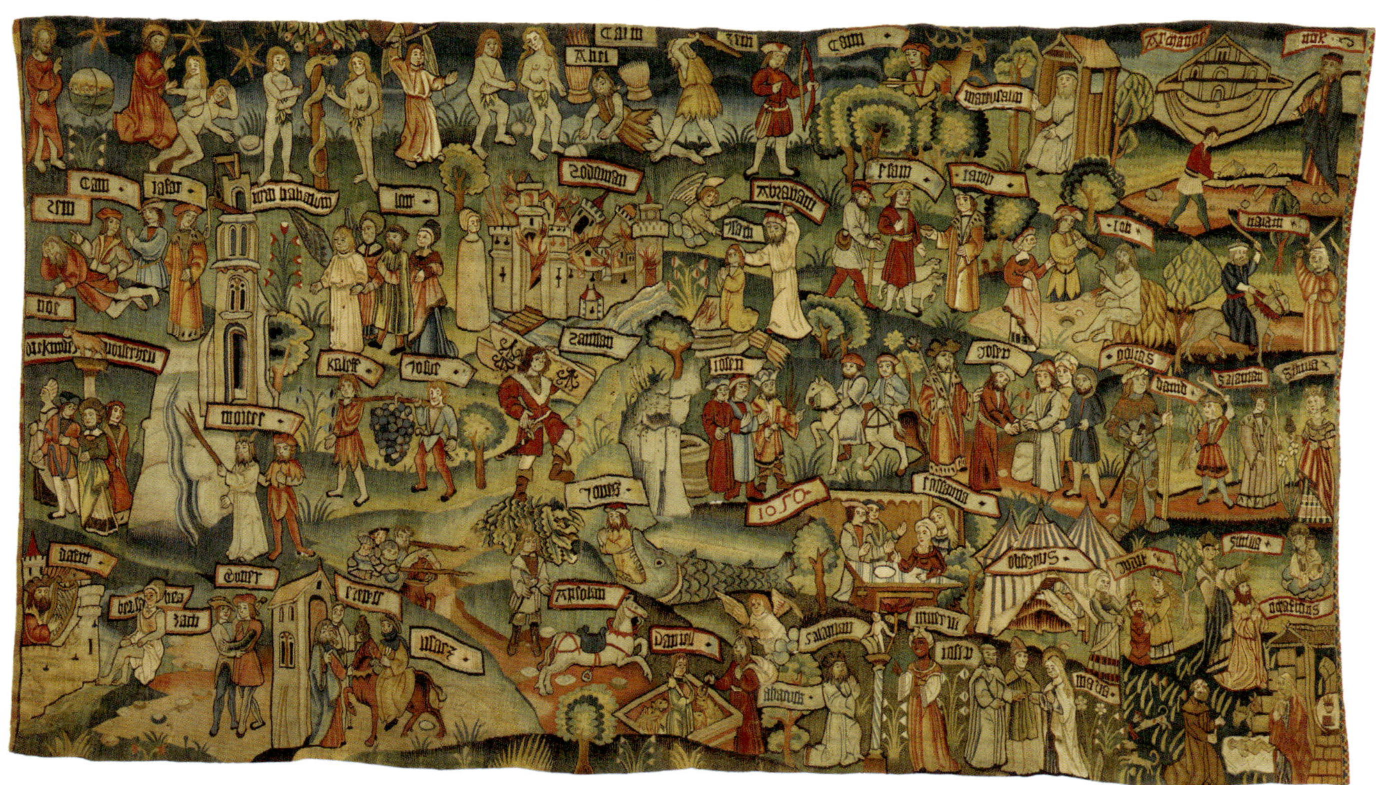

The Bible Tapestry, about 1550

Made in Germany
Wool, linen, silk, metal thread
159 cm x 276 cm
46.20

The anonymous designer has arranged 32 Old Testament and two New Testament stories from the Creation of Adam and Eve (top left) to the birth of Jesus Christ (bottom right) in chronological order in this extraordinary tapestry. Each story in this tapestry has been labelled individually and was probably copied from contemporary and earlier woodcuts, including the *Biblia Pauperum*, or 'Pauper's Bible', first published in 1460–70. In a period when the Bible was generally only available in Latin and the majority of people were not taught to read, this tapestry was probably used as a teaching aid by priests.

Object in Focus

The Luttrell Table Carpet, about 1514–80
Made in Southern Netherlands, now Belgium,
or England
Wool, silk, metal threads
193 cm x 553 cm
47.3

In the 1500s carpets were expensive so were often placed on tables rather than on the floor, to be removed and replaced with linen if food was served. Table carpets were made in various techniques, including knotted pile and embroidery, as well as tapestry. Many were bought ready-made, but the majority of surviving examples are one-off commissions

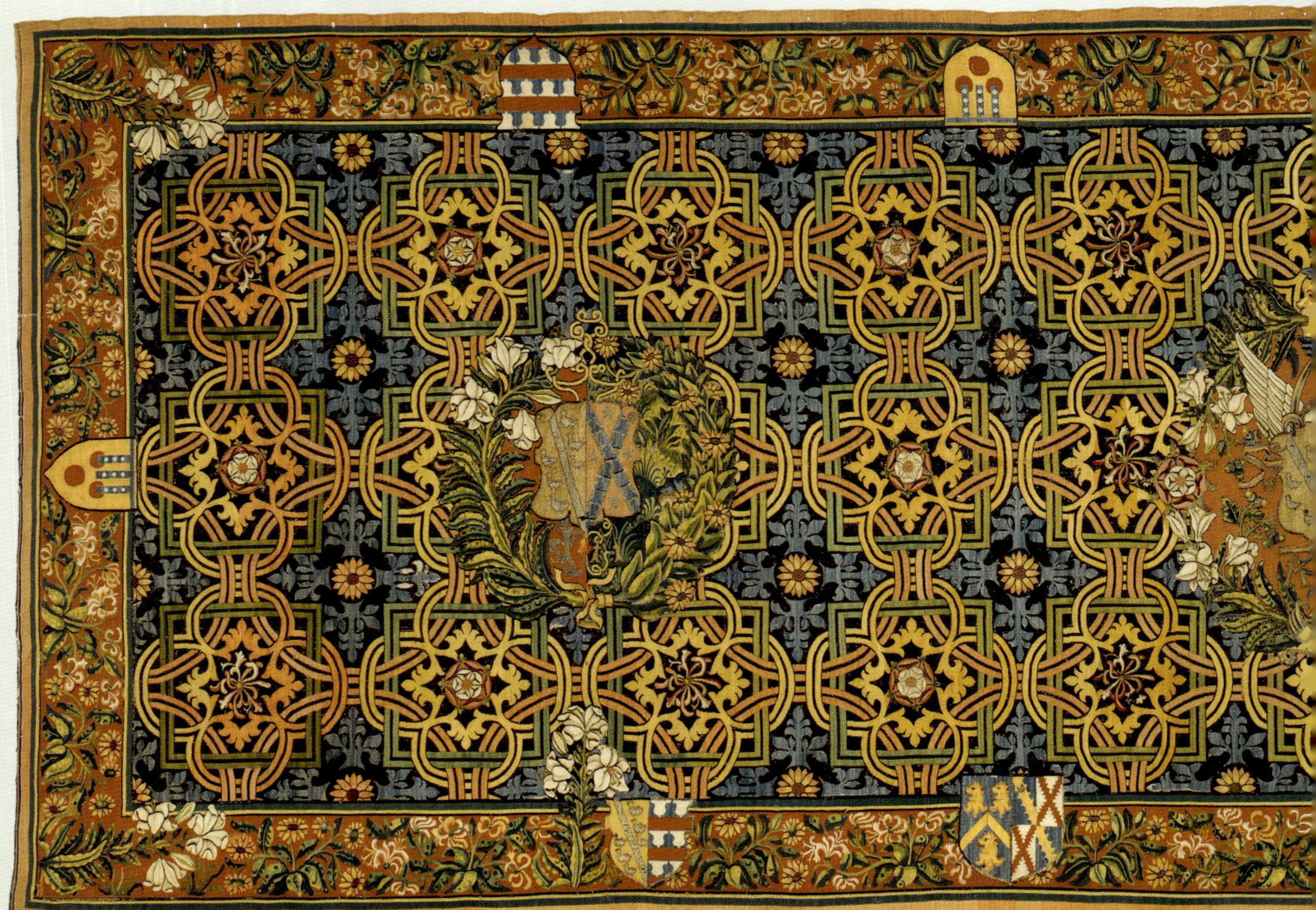

with designs that incorporate the owner's family coats of arms. This table carpet was made for Sir Andrew Luttrell (1484–1538) of Dunster and Quantoxhead, whose arms in the centre are shown impaled with that of his wife Margaret Wyndham (d. 1580), who he married in 1514. The arms of his parents, Sir Hugh Luttrell (d. 1521) and Margaret Hill (d. 1508) on the left and his paternal grandparents, Sir James Luttrell (1426/7–1461) and Elizabeth Courtenay (d. 1493), on the right. Wider family connections are represented on the arms displayed around the border. This bespoke table carpet was a prized possession and as such was specifically named as 'her best and longest carpet' in Margaret's will dated 9 March 1580 in which she bequeathed it to her daughter, Mrs Margaret Edgecumbe.

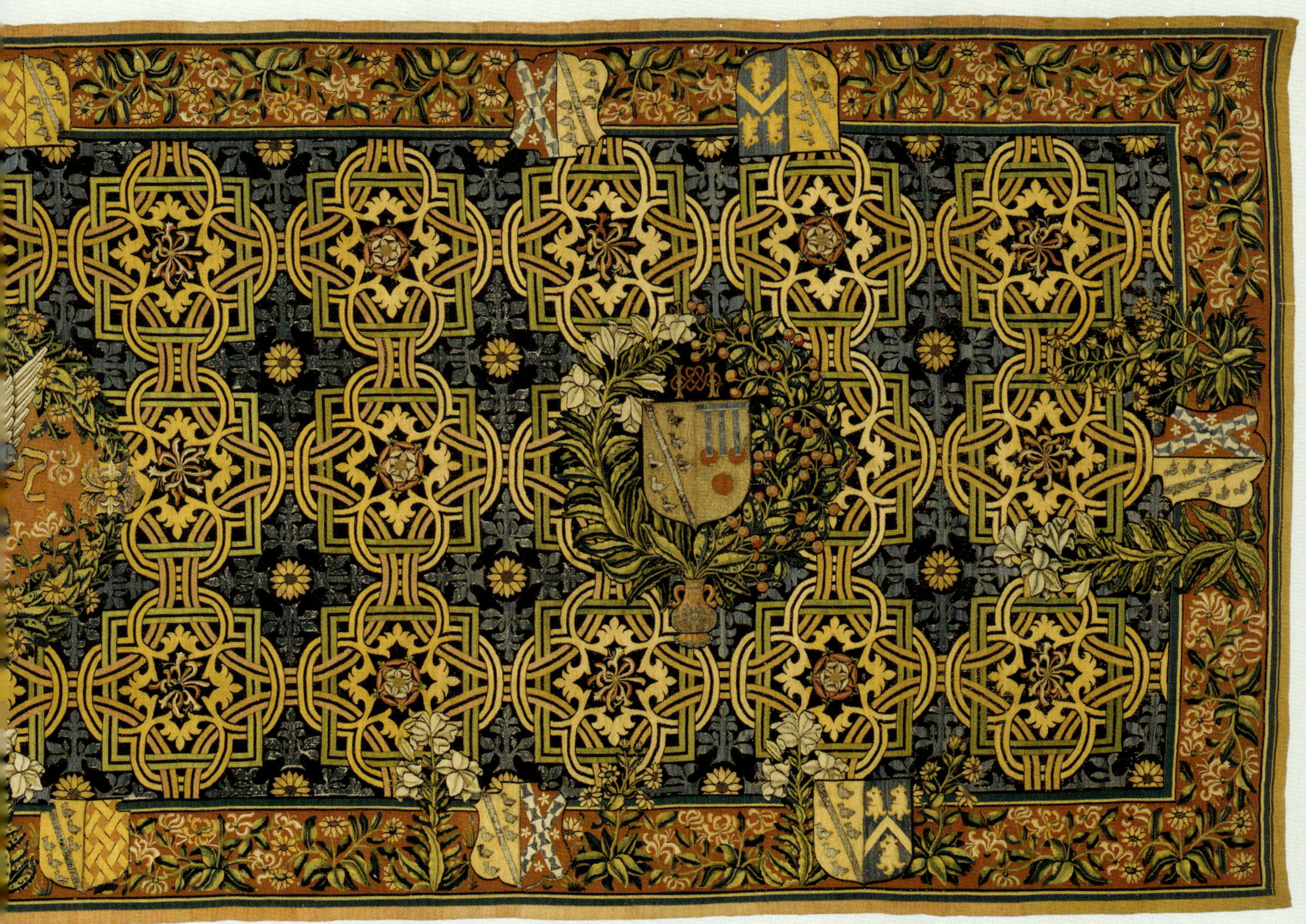

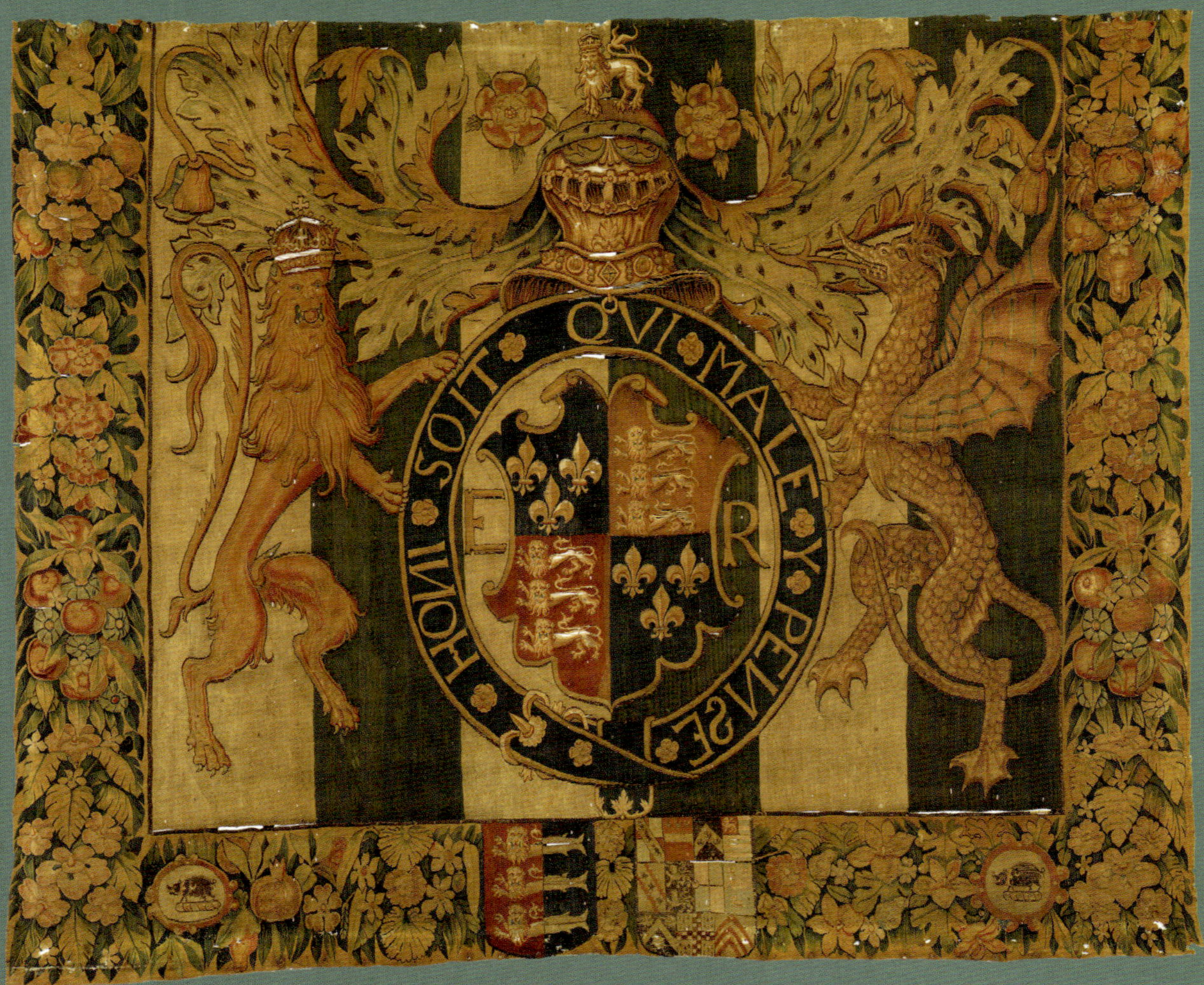

The Great Yarmouth Cloth of Estate with Tudor Arms, about 1547–94
Possibly made in Enghien, Hainaut,
Southern Netherlands, now Belgium, or England
Wool, silk
209 cm x 252 cm
47.4

Cloths of Estate are ceremonial hangings that represent the status and power of an important figure and often feature that person's coat of arms. Here it is the royal arms with the shield showing three lions passant gardant quartered with three fleur-de-lys surrounded by the Order of the Garter and supporters representing England and Wales against the Tudor colours of green and white. The 'E' and 'R' either side are for Edward VI (1537–53) or Elizabeth I of England (1533–1603). The tapestry was hung originally above the bailiffs' bar in the Heyning Chamber of the Great Yarmouth Tolhouse to represent the law of the monarch during court proceedings.

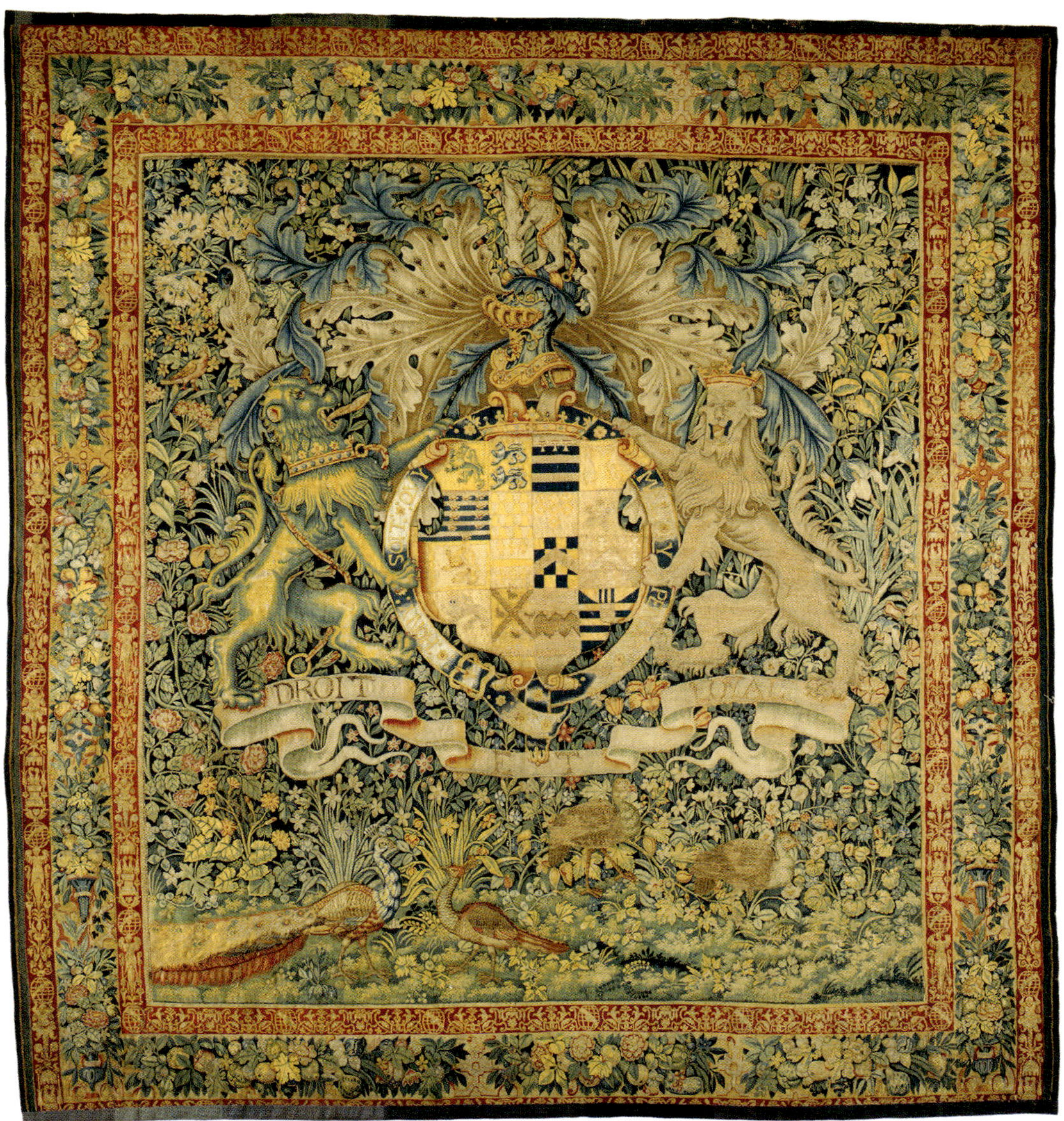

Verdure with the Arms of Robert Dudley, Earl of Leicester, before 1585

Made in Southern Netherlands, now Belgium,
or England
Wool, silk
292 cm x 263 cm
47.1

Robert Dudley, 1st Earl of Leicester (1532–88) was the favourite courtier of Queen Elizabeth I of England. His father, John Dudley, 1st Duke of Northumberland, had been executed in 1553 and his family lost the title. Robert was later made 1st Earl of Leicester in 1564.

This is one of three tapestries commissioned by Dudley that show his coat of arms against a verdure or foliage background. One of these, also in the Burrell Collection, is woven with a similar design. The third, which is double the width and shows his arms between cartouches with fountains, is now in the Victoria and Albert Museum, London.

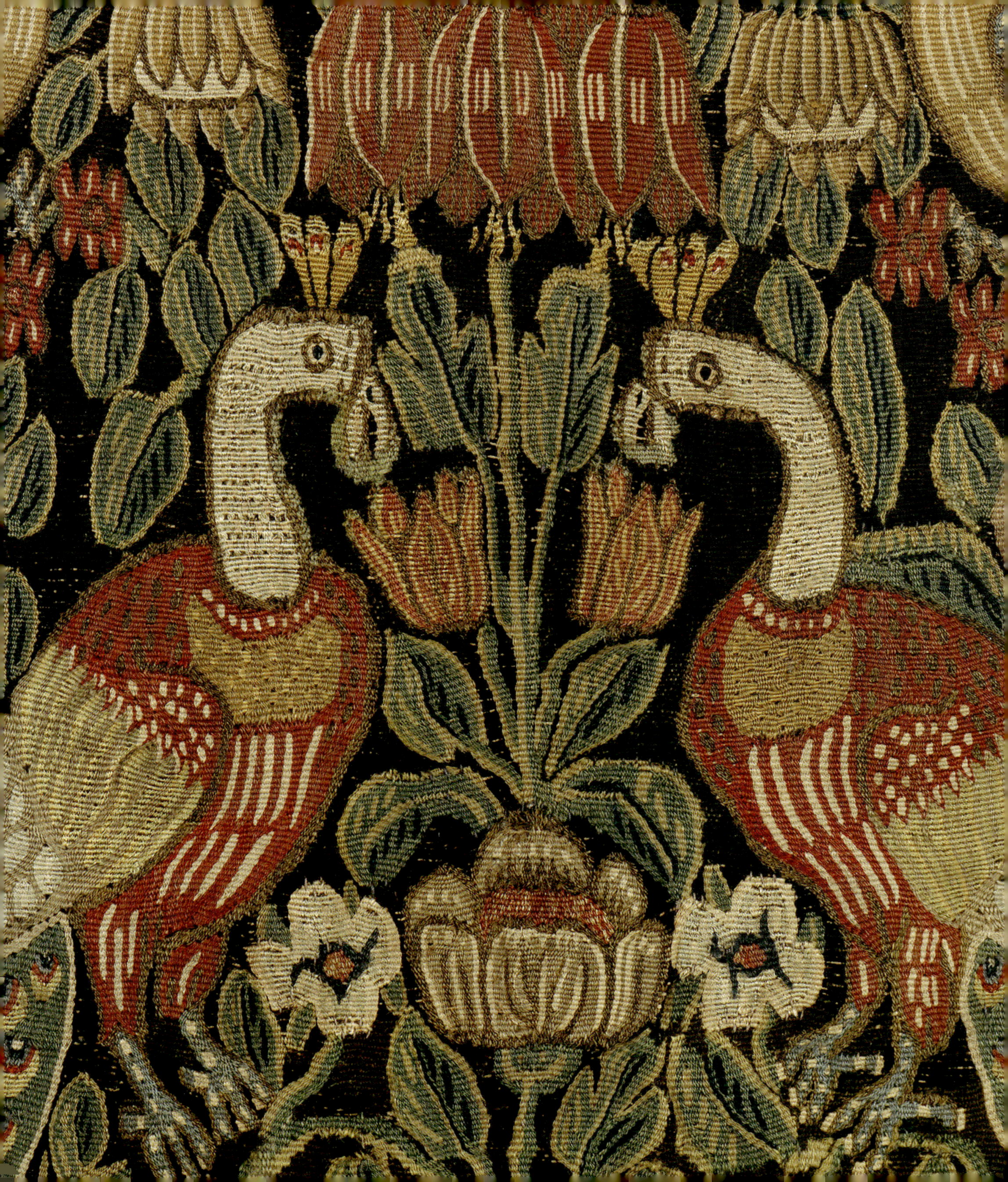

Seventeenth-century Tapestries

Grand large-scale tapestries, based on cartoons by leading Baroque artists, continued to be woven in the Southern Netherlands during the 1600s, but there were new competitors. In London a tapestry workshop was established at Mortlake in 1619; in France Jean-Baptiste Colbert (1619–83), minister of finance for King Louis XIV (1643–1715), founded the Gobelins tapestry factory in Paris in 1661 and another at Beauvais in 1664.

Meanwhile, weavers who had emigrated from the Southern Netherlands during the civil wars and religious persecution of the 1560s and 1570s had settled and opened small workshops in England, the Dutch Republic, northern Germany and Denmark. They produced tapestries that appealed to the purses and taste of the growing numbers of wealthy merchants and professionals, including panels for upholstered chairs and cushion covers.

Sir William Burrell's taste did not generally favour large French Baroque tapestries, so while he did collect seventeenth-century tapestries, they were of the small, domestic type. The subjects on these include Biblical stories as well as decorative designs of flowers and birds, which often complement the English domestic embroideries Burrell was acquiring.

An avid collector, Burrell was also a generous lender throughout his lifetime. He was a member of the organizing committee for the Glasgow International Exhibition in 1901, to which he lent a number of paintings, tapestries and embroideries to the Fine Art Section, including *Faith, Hope and Charity.* This commitment to lending for public view continued throughout the remainder of his life, with long-term loans of his tapestries to museums, colleges and cathedrals in Britain. *The Boar Hunt* was lent to The Bowes Museum, the Fitzwilliam received several including *Hector's Tomb* and the Victoria and Albert Museum, London had the *Verdure with the Arms of Robert Dudley, Earl of Leicester.* After he gifted his collection to Glasgow in 1944 these loans were returned and today form one of the most significant parts of the Burrell Collection and are of international importance.

Opposite: this cushion cover was an early acquisition for Burrell, who not only displayed it in his home on Great Western Terrace, but also lent it to several loan exhibitions during the early 1900s. *Two Parrots and Two Peacocks with Flowers* (detail; see also p. 70).

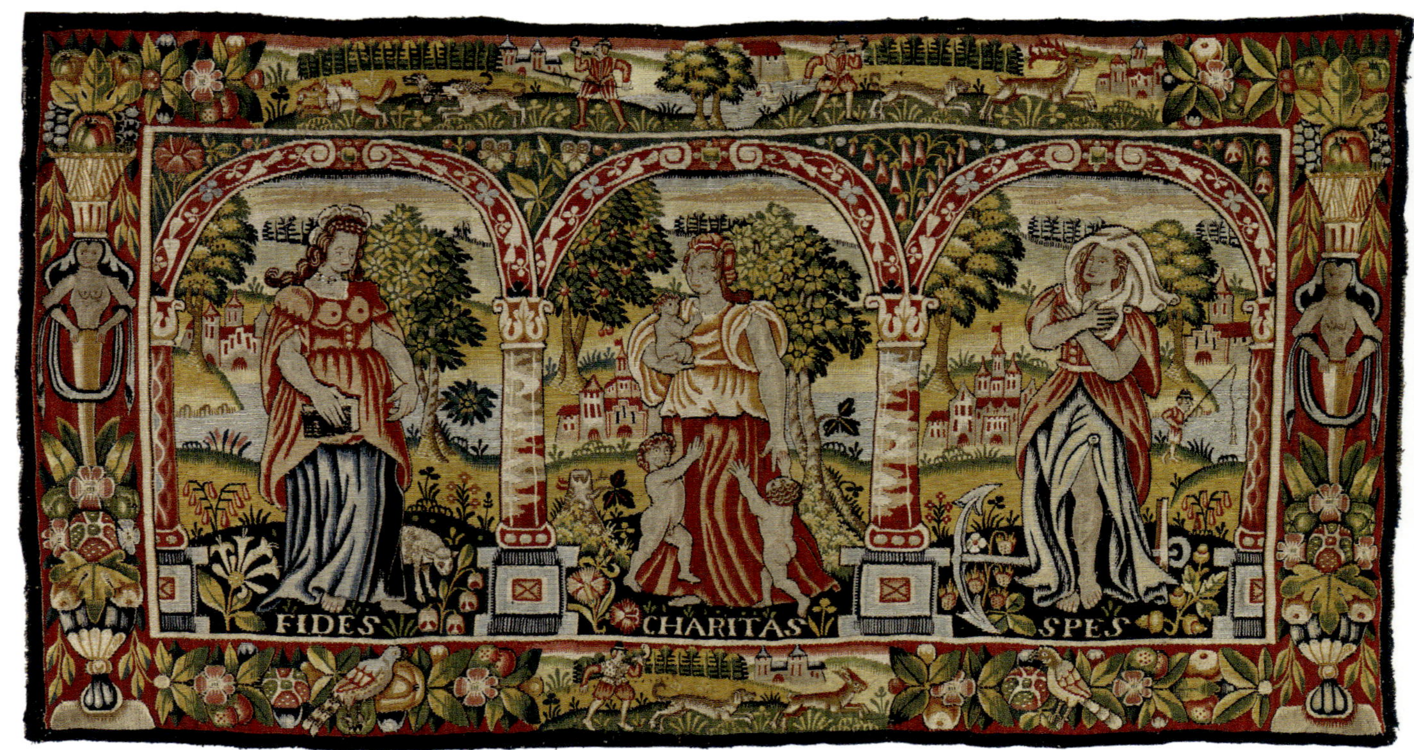

The Theological Virtues: Faith, Hope and Charity, about 1620

Possibly made in London, England
Wool, silk
54 cm x 99 cm
47.19

Faith (*fides*), Hope (*spes*) and Charity (*charitas*) are the three theological virtues in the Christian church. They are often personified as women identifiable by their attributes; here Faith is shown with a Bible and lamb; Hope with an anchor and Charity with three children.

This was an early purchase for William Burrell, who lent it to the Glasgow International Exhibition in 1901. The design appears to have been popular as several versions exist in other collections, including one bought by William Hesketh Lever (1851–1925), a contemporary collector to Burrell, which is now in the Lady Lever Art Gallery, Port Sunlight, England.

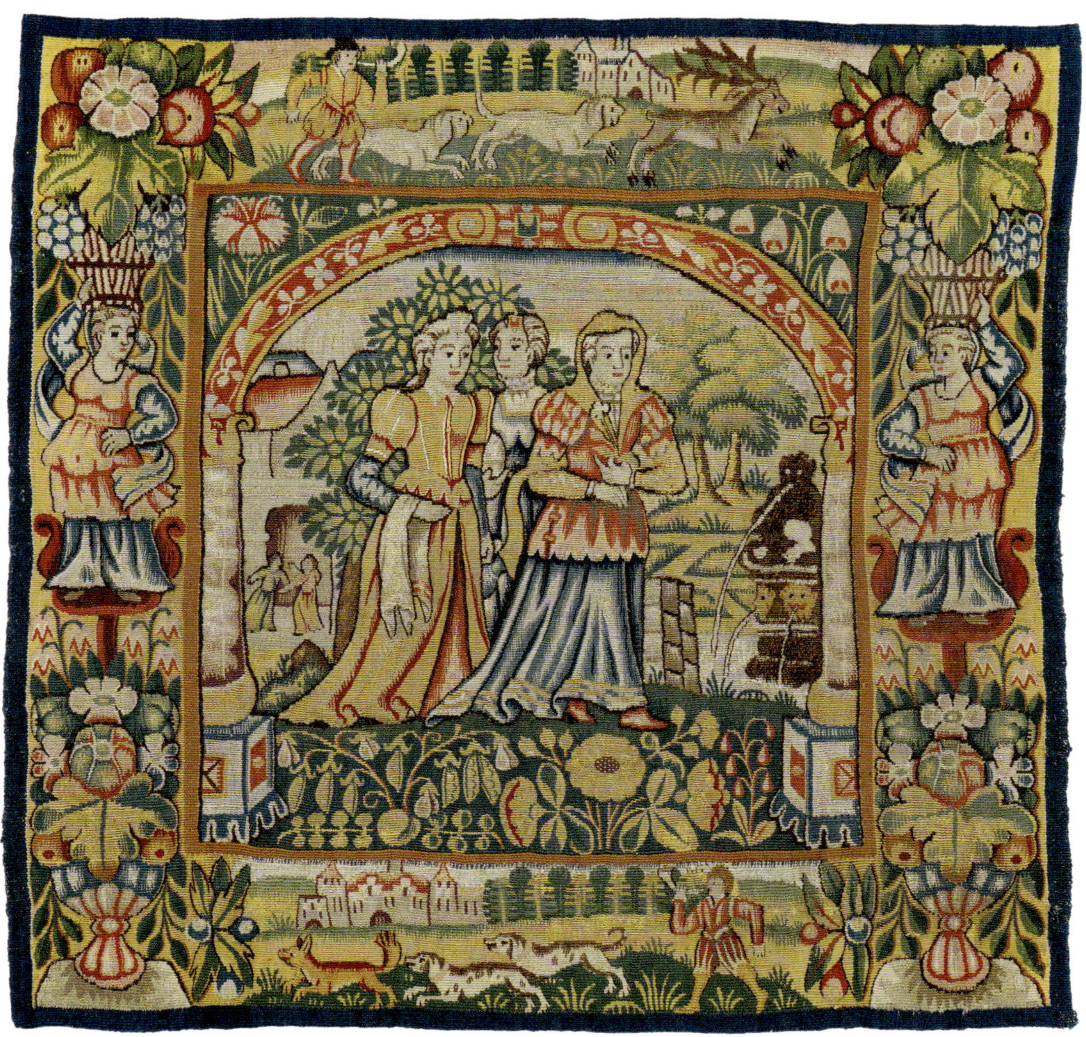

Susanna and the Elders: Susanna on Her Way to the Baths, about 1625
Possibly made in London, England
Wool, silk
51 cm x 52 cm
47.9

The size and proportions of small tapestries, like this example, suggest they were designed to be made up into cushion covers. William Burrell collected several of these tapestries, including one full six-piece set and four other pieces, which show Susanna and the Elders, and some showing scenes from the Story of Jacob. The layout of this type of English tapestry appears to follow a set template of a Biblical scene set within an arch. The surrounding border with hunting scenes along the top and bottom was a popular English design and is found on contemporary embroideries too, including the Bradford Table Carpet, now in the Victoria and Albert Museum, London.

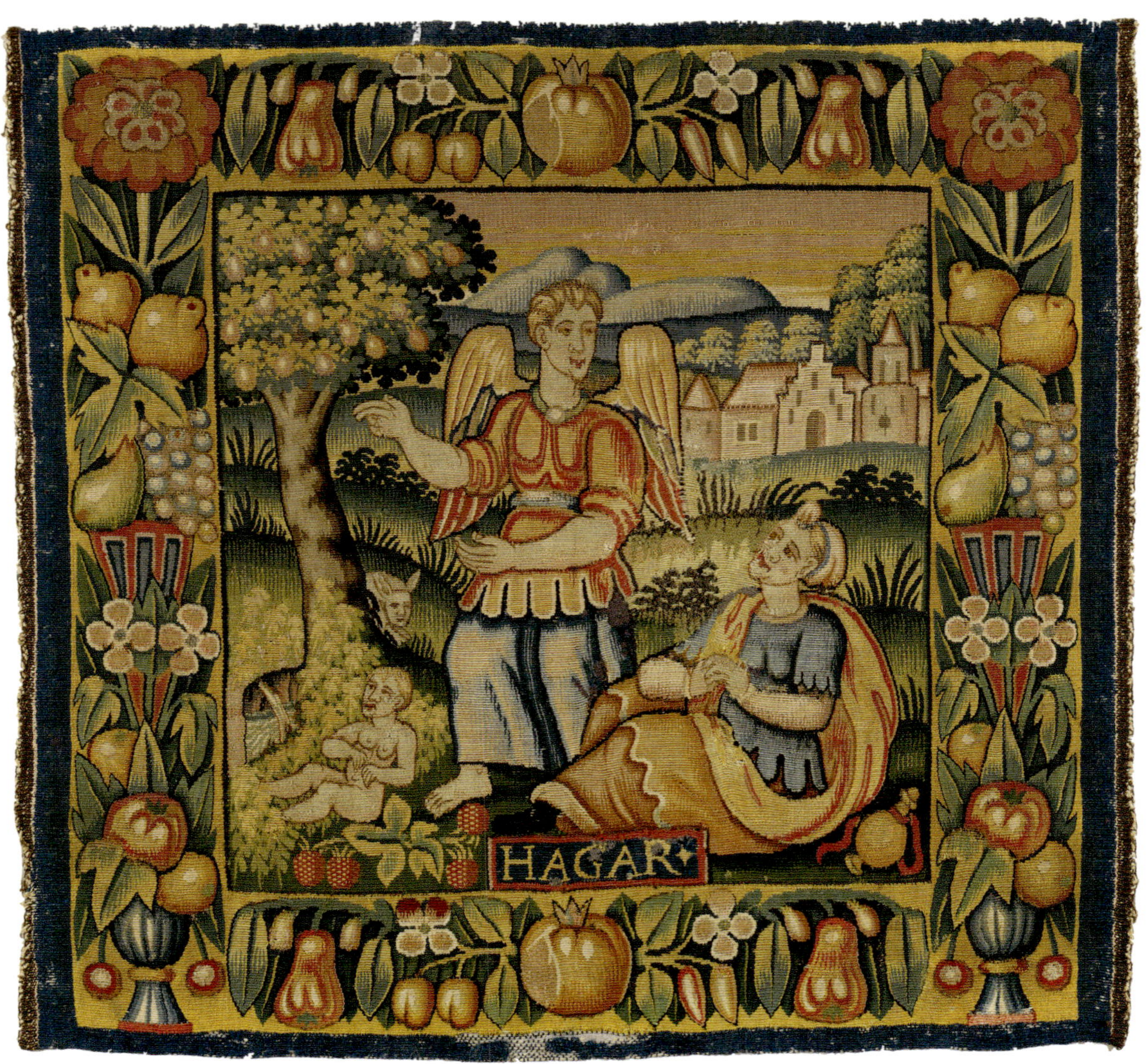

Hagar, about 1600–30
Made in Germany
Wool, linen, silk
55 cm x 60 cm
47.30

Hagar and her son Ishmael, cast out by their master Abraham, have exhausted their supply of food and drink, but just as they begin to despair an angel appears and points them towards a nearby spring.

This type of cushion cover was made by Flemish weavers who had left the Southern Netherlands and emigrated to northern Germany as a result of religious or political persecution. They are similar in size and subject matter to cushion covers made by other Flemish weavers who moved to England, although the style of the design is different.

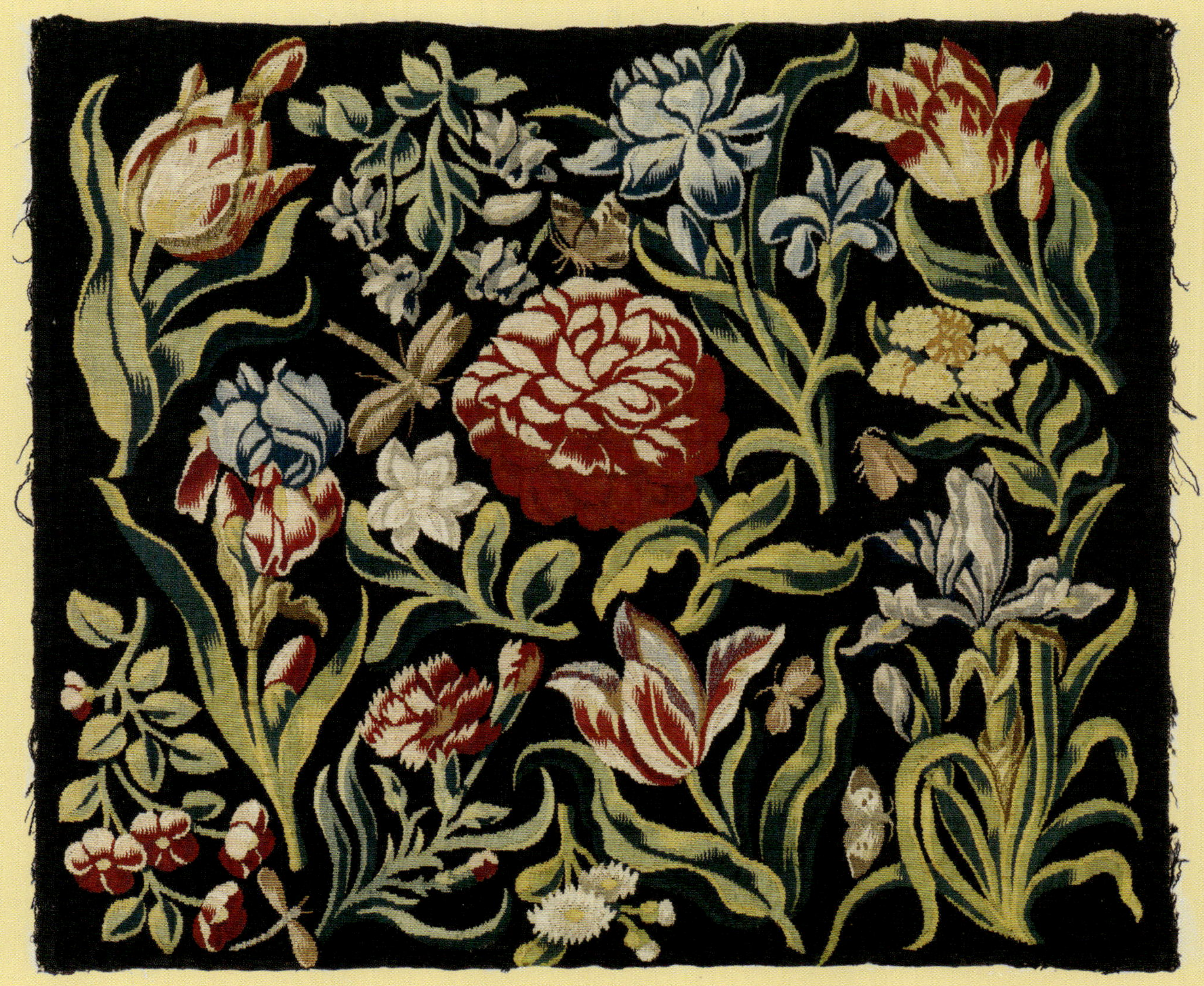

Floral Cushion Cover, about 1650
Made in the Dutch Republic, now the Netherlands
Wool, linen, silk
52 cm x 60 cm
47.29.a

A profusion of naturalistic flowers are strewn across cushion covers woven in the Northern Netherlands, reflecting the Dutch passion for collecting flowers, particularly tulips, at this period. The blooms are set against a plain dark background that shows off their varied colours and shapes. Contemporary botanical publications featured both plain and hand-coloured engravings of flowers that inspired still life paintings and textile designs, both on tapestries and embroideries.

This is one of two pairs of panels originally designed as cushion covers, that were mounted into a folding screen in about 1750.

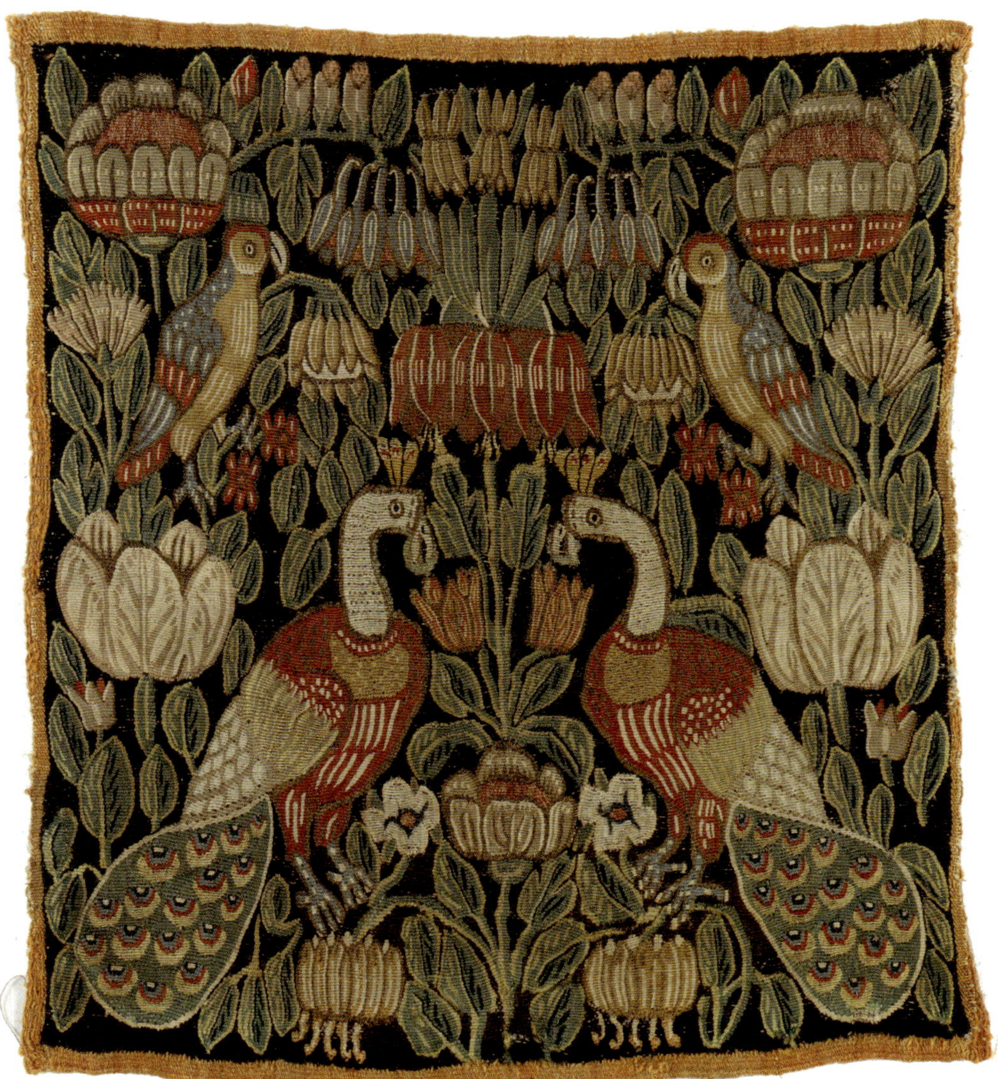

Birds, such as parrots and peacocks, alongside flowers are popular motifs found on small tapestry cushion covers woven in the workshops near Hamburg, Germany, and neighbouring Schleswig-Holstein, a region spanning what is now northern Germany and southern Denmark. The flat, linear motifs without shading colours have a folk-like appearance.

This and a couple of other similar style tapestries were lent by William Burrell along with a number of needlework pieces in his collection to the *Exhibition of Ancient and Modern Embroidery and Needlecraft* at The Glasgow School of Art in 1916.

Two Parrots and Two Peacocks with Flowers,
about 1675–1725
Made in Germany or Denmark
Wool, linen, silk
58 cm x 52 cm
47.39

The *Ports de Mer* or 'Sea Ports'
series of tapestries were made
at the French royal tapestry
manufactory founded in Beauvais
by Louis XIV's minister of finance,
Jean-Baptiste Colbert, in 1664.
These designs featuring a variety
of birds in the foreground of
different sea ports were so popular
the cartoons continued to be
used for over 40 years.

As well as leaving his collection
to Glasgow, Sir William Burrell
also left a sum of money for
additional items to be bought for
the collection. This tapestry was
purchased by the Burrell Trustees
in 1971.

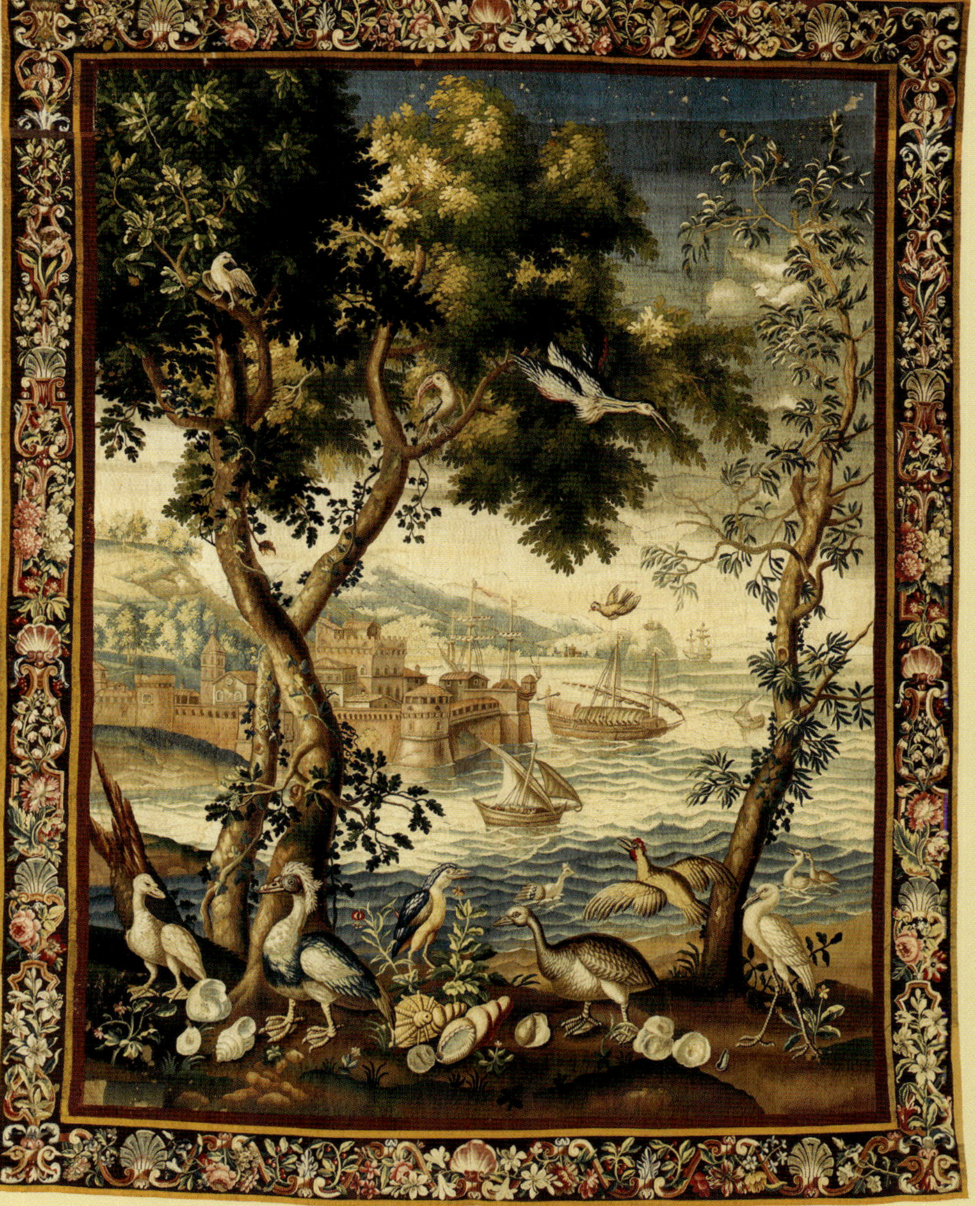

Seaport, about 1695–1737
Designed by Adrien Campion and J. van den Kerchove,
made under the directorship of Philippe Behagle,
the Filleul brothers or Noel Antoine Merou, Beauvais,
France
Wool, silk
350 cm x 272 cm
47.45

Further Reading

Martin Bellamy and Isobel MacDonald, *William Burrell: A Collector's Life*, Glasgow Museums and Birlinn, Edinburgh, 2022. Biography of William Burrell, his life, collection and legacy.

Thomas P. Campbell, *Tapestry in the Renaissance: Art and Magnificence*, Metropolitan Museum of Art, New York, 2002. Exhibition catalogue. Accessible introduction to Renaissance tapestries.

Elizabeth Cleland and Lorraine Karafel, *Tapestries from the Burrell Collection*, Philip Wilson Publishers in association with Glasgow Museums, London, 2017. Full academic catalogue of all the European tapestries in the Burrell Collection.

Heinrich Göbel, *Wandteppiche*, Klinkhardt and Biermann, Leipzig, 1923–34. Three volumes. Key early study on tapestries including ones later purchased by Burrell.

Betty Kurth, *Die deutschen Bildteppiche des Mittelalters*, A Schroll, Vienna, 1926. Key early study on medieval German tapestries including ones later purchased by Burrell.

Anna Rapp Buri and Monica Stucky-Schrer, *Zahm und Wild: Basler und Strassburger Bildteppiche des 15. Jahrhunderts*, Philipp von Zabern, 1990. Key study on fifteenth-century Basel and Strasbourg tapestries.

W.G. Thomson, *A History of Tapestry from the Earliest Times until the Present Day*, 1906, third revised edition EP Publishing, East Ardsley, 1973. Accessible introduction to tapestries.